# ENGLISH FAIRS AND MARKETS

# ENGLISH FAIRS and MARKETS

WILLIAM ADDISON

*with illustrations by*

BARBARA JONES

LONDON

B. T. BATSFORD LTD

'For every man hath business or desire, such as it is'

*First published* 1953

MADE AND PRINTED IN GREAT BRITAIN BY WILLIAM CLOWES
AND SONS LTD, LONDON AND BECCLES, FOR THE PUBLISHERS
B. T. BATSFORD LTD
4 FITZHARDINGE STREET, PORTMAN SQUARE, LONDON, W.1.

# PREFACE

**B**OUND up as they are with the most vital concerns of our social history, it seems odd that so little has been written about fairs and markets in England. The first book on fairs was Henry Morley's *Memoirs of Bartholomew Fair*, published in 1859. In 1883 it was followed by Cornelius Walford's *Fairs, Past and Present*, which dealt with the legislation controlling fairs and markets and traced in detail the rise and fall of the two greatest, Sturbridge and Bartholomew. Other mediæval fairs have been the subjects of monographs; but it was not until 1936, when the Rev. R. W. Muncey's *Our Old English Fairs* was published, that we got a book on fairs in general.

Even less has been written about markets in general. Several admirable and scholarly articles on those of single counties have been contributed to the proceedings of learned societies; their legal aspect has been dealt with more than once; their economic aspect has been the subject of two exhaustive surveys, that of the Royal Commission on Market Rights and Tolls, which published its Report in 1889–91, and the second and more specialized survey made by the Ministry of Agriculture and Fisheries for the publications of 1927. None of these, however, are for the general reader. Nor do they give the student of social history a comprehensive view of fairs and markets in relation to the life and character of England and the English people, which is the purpose of this book. The truth is that history as well as commerce needs its middlemen, particularly in a subject in which history and commerce combine.

Fairs and markets were frequently granted together in the Middle Ages. They were usually granted to the same lord of the manor, whether lay or clerical, and they have always had much in common. With both there is a chartered concourse of buyers and sellers at a given time and place, with the primary distinction that fairs have an annual, markets a weekly, regulation. Yet they are a couple who came together, as it

v

were, by marriage, not birth. The market as an institution is
entirely the product of economic need, with regulations
governed by civil law. We have an extreme instance of this
at Hemel Hempstead in Hertfordshire, where the inhabitants
were incorporated solely for the purpose of holding the market
granted to them in 1539. Fairs on the other hand may be
romantic in origin and are governed by customs and circumstances in which the rhyme is usually more apparent than the
reason. The Royal Commission's Report described the fair as
"originally an institution derived from ancient tribal and
national usages expanding in later times with the growth of
the royal prerogative and the increasing necessities of commerce." The festive element in the fair, which is lacking in
the market, is the most obvious survival of these "ancient
tribal and national usages," and the one to which society has
clung most tenaciously. According to the Ministry of Agriculture and Fisheries' survey, there were still about 1,500
fairs held each year in England and Wales in 1927, and we
may be sure that it was the festive element that kept most of
them going.

Apart from their inherent interest, fairs and markets
concern everyone because they have conditioned—we might
almost say controlled—the development of the English town.
Fairs were too infrequent to produce permanent memorials;
but it was from the rows of booths ranged to form streets,
with a broad main thoroughfare leading to the abbey or
castle gateway, that the town took its shape. The effect of
markets is obvious. Whether as at Malmesbury, Abingdon,
Chichester, and innumerable other places its site is marked
by a splendid cross, or only by an ancient stone such as everywhere marked points of assembly at one time, it is in the market and the church that the English town is nucleated. In
writing this book, therefore, I have tried to bring out the
topographical as well as the social implications of fairs and
markets, because without an adequate idea of these we cannot
hope to appreciate the part they have played in English life,
or even grasp their character.

W. A.

Loughton, Essex.
*Martinmas*, 1952.

# CONTENTS

# ACKNOWLEDGMENT

THE author gratefully acknowledges his indebtedness to all who have helped with information, particularly the many city and borough librarians who have so readily placed their local collections at his disposal— unlocking their cupboards and reaching down neatly tied bundles to demonstrate again and again that there are still a great many good things wrapped up in small parcels!

# CHAPTER I

# Fairs and their Origins

THE old English fair, notwithstanding the richness of its mediæval lore and economic importance, now lives in the popular mind as the kind of event depicted by Hogarth and Rowlandson, and described by such writers as Hardy, Borrow, and Defoe. That is to say, the last impressions remain and the rest are forgotten. Not that these should be disparaged. Even to our day the village fair has commonly been the social event of the year—livelier even than Christmas. "The scent of bruised grass," a neighbour of mine confided while mowing her lawn, "always reminds me of Melford Fair." She was a Suffolk woman, separated from her native Long Melford by years as well as miles, but the spell still worked!

It was the same everywhere. The seasons themselves seemed to wait on the fairs. "On Heffel Fair Day," the people of Sussex used to say, "the old woman lets the cuckoo out." Spring, they meant, came in with Heathfield Fair. As for autumn, the people of Devon will tell you that hazel-nuts become slip-shell on Denbury Fair Day,[1] and should never

---

[1] 19th September.

be picked earlier. There is no end to such lore, to say nothing of the curious customs and ceremonies connected with fairs. Yet for all the excitement of their naphtha flares, their fabulous beasts, gingerbread stalls, and what-not, these fairs of the last generation, and of many before it, were only the after-glow of the fairs that had been.

Hardy, perhaps, was the last to describe from personal knowledge an ancient fair, which while not in its prime still retained much of its original purpose and character. "Greenhill," he tells us in *Far From the Madding Crowd*, was "the Nijni Novgorod of South Wessex; and the busiest, merriest day of the whole statute number was the day of the sheep fair." He was describing the great September fair on Woodbury Hill, near Bere Regis, held by right of a charter granted by Henry III in 1216, which at one time lasted from the 18th to the 25th of the month. Each day had its appointed business. The first was kept for wholesale transactions. On the second, when the gentry attended, the scene would be similar to that at a county agricultural show in our own day. The third was the popular day. The fourth—the sheep day— was the one described by Hardy. Shepherds, he says, might start from home "two or three days, or even a week, before the fair, driving their charges a few miles each day—not more than ten or twelve—and resting them at night in hired fields by the wayside." We can imagine the scene, and see how impracticable it would be to have such flocks on the road to-day.

"Greenhill" had its days for horses and cattle, a "pack and penny" day and various others, each with both its regulated sales and traditional fare. Roast pork, for example, came into season in Dorset at Woodbury Hill Fair, while the special delicacy was Poole oysters. Yet even this most popular of all the Wessex fairs petered out when regular markets and auction marts in Dorchester and smaller towns made it redundant. Sheep were sold at Hardy's "Greenhill" for the last time in 1906.[1] It was, in fact, a late survival. Indeed, fairs had been on the wane since the fifteenth century. Before that the scene must have been lively indeed, when even at village fairs chapmen and minstrels, monks and peasants,

[1] *Notes and Queries*, 10th Series, viii, p. 250.

after travelling like Chaucer's pilgrims would elbow their way to the village cross, eager to be present when the lord of the manor's steward stepped out on the sounding of a horn or the ringing of a bell to proclaim the fair. And it is surprising how many of these ceremonial openings have survived to our own day in all the glory of their mediæval pageantry, particularly in the Catholic west and north.

Woodbury Hill Fair, like numerous others, was incalculably older than its charter. "This yearly gathering," says Hardy, "was upon the summit of a hill which retained in good preservation the remains of an ancient earthwork, consisting of a huge rampart and entrenchment of an oval form encircling the top of the hill, though somewhat broken down here and there. To each of the two chief openings on opposite sides a winding road ascended, and the level green space of ten or fifteen acres enclosed by the bank was the site of the fair." The site is significant. Many fairs are found near prehistoric earthworks, or where they are obviously the survival of a vanished community to which the fair had been vital, supplying, as it did, salt to preserve the meat on which the people lived throughout the winter, millstones for grinding their corn, iron for implements, and tar for sheep-scab.

Of various speculations on the institution of fairs in general the most credible is that of Sir Henry Maine, who in *Village Communities in the East and West* describes the rudiments of social life in small autonomous communities, each cultivating its own little clearing, living constantly at war with its neighbours and always in fear of attack, and suggests that in such a society places for parley had to be found, which in course of time came to be regarded as neutral ground, and therefore suitable points for barter and the proclamation of inter-tribal laws. Here, in more settled times, a new village might spring up and replace the older settlements, the offspring, as it were, of their union. A similar connection between trade and neutrality is mooted by Sir John Lubbock in the *Origin of Civilisation*; and we certainly know that the practice of proclaiming new laws at fairs is common to many countries. It was the Roman custom. It was the custom in Ireland—although there the laws were taken about as seriously as the roundabouts! And in England new laws were always proclaimed at fairs in

3

the Middle Ages on the authority of a king's writ to the sheriff. As for the association of fairs with neutrality, we have an illustration of this in the Domesday account of Dover. The 1889 Report of the Royal Commission on Fairs and Markets, in mentioning this particular instance of the *Treva Regis*, or "Peace of the Fair," reminds us of the Norse saga of Grettir, the outlawed athlete, who came to a Spring festival, or fair, in disguise, and when invited to wrestle agreed to do so provided the "peace" could be proclaimed. When this had been done he threw off his disguise, and although the contestants were enraged to find that they had been outwitted, there was no question of punishing him. As the peace had been proclaimed he must enjoy its protection.

Every county must have records of this truce at fair-time. I noticed a seventeenth-century instance of it at Thaxted in an Essex Sessions Roll a few days ago:

> "We present that the Sunday before Whytsonday last one Tayler of the same towne dyd lodge in his howse at the same tyme, then being the fayere daye, the number of thyrtye roges and stute beggers which one Paule Chapman constable there dyd nomber and ponysshed none of them."[1]

But the most important persons to be protected were the merchants. For their safety the first Statute of Winchester ordered bushes, woods, and dykes to be cleared for 200 feet on either side of the highway, and when charters were granted to towns it was usual to insert such clauses as that in Hubert de Burgh's to Montgomery: "that all merchants shall come safely to the said town with their merchandise, doing the right and usual customs, and shall be under the earl's protection in coming, tarrying, and returning."[2] On the other hand, the number of these safe conducts reminds us how dangerous travel to fairs and markets was.

So while we may assume that trading began as a by-product of peace or neutrality, it produced its own conflicts of sharp practices, which were in some ways fostered by the very conditions so essential for its progress. It is for this reason, no doubt, that we find Hermes, or Mercury, figuring

---

[1] ERO/QSR. 27/5.
[2] Ch. Rolls, 12 Henry III m. 2.

as patron of trade, god of boundaries, and protector of thieves —protector, that is to say, of the pickpockets who have always flourished at fairs, as well as of such cunning rogues as Grettir, and such stout beggars as those who cheated the people of Thaxted. It is, in fact, surprising to find how adroitly Hermes performs all the offices of the guardian spirit of fairs and markets, and how suitably he was trained for them. He was born in Arcadia, and qualified as thief by stealing fifty oxen from the sacred herd of the gods. He invented the lyre. He presided over the gymnastic exercises which have always been connected with fairs. He was the messenger of the gods. Homer makes him the patron of eloquence, and there has certainly been more than enough of that at fairs. He had the gift of interpreting dreams, and was thus the sanctified forerunner of the fortune-tellers and soothsayers who have wheedled the last shilling out of the pockets of the credulous from his day to ours. It was he who invented the dice. And on the honourable side of the account, it was he to whom travellers turned for protection, because he was the guardian of roads, with the pillar stones that evolved into market crosses for his symbol. He was also the patron of public treaties. Hermes is thus behind everything connected with fairs—he has the cock for a symbol because he loves fighting, the purse because he guards travellers, the ram and the goblet because he was the director of sacrifice and religious ceremony.

This last of his attributes reminds us of a tradition in the history of fairs that might at first appear to have no connection with their mercantile function. It is often said that fairs have lost their original character and degenerated into Saturnalian festivals. Yet the very term of this abuse hints at the paradox that their end was their beginning. Many have in fact reverted to an earlier condition. In symbolic language, they have lost the purse, but the cock is still there. As for the ram and goblet, these represent the origin of most of our English fairs, because while the first fairs of all would come into being as Sir Henry Maine suggests, those of later ages had different causes. To explain the fairs of a second order we cannot do better than read T. F. Dexter's book, *The Pagan Origin of Fairs*, in which he traces his particular group back to those heathen funeral games performed annually at the

burial place of a dead hero, which have their Greek counterparts in the Olympian games. Later again the shrine of a
Christian saint was substituted for the grave of the pagan
hero, which led many to believe that fairs had a common and
universal origin in the assembling of pilgrims at the shrines
of Christian saints, although there should be no difficulty in
seeing the error of this if it is remembered that fairs are found
in non-Christian countries, and are pre-Christian in the rest.
To account for their obvious connection with so many Christian shrines in England we have only to recall how Gregory
the Great wrote to Bishop Mellitus in 601: "I have, upon
mature deliberation on the affairs of the English, determined
that the temples of the idols in that nation ought not to be
destroyed. Let holy water be made and sprinkled in the said
temples; let altars be erected, and relics placed, that seeing
their temples are not destroyed, the people may the more
familiarly resort to the places to which they have been
accustomed. And because they have been used to slaughter
many oxen in the sacrifices to devils, some solemnity must
be exchanged for them on this account, as that on the day
of the dedication, or the nativities of the holy martyrs, whose
relics are there deposited. They may build themselves huts
of the boughs of trees about those churches, which have been
turned to that use from temples, and celebrate the solemnity
with religious feasting, and no more offer beasts to the devil,
but kill cattle to the praise of God in their eating, and return
thanks to the giver of all things for their sustenance." [1]
Gregory knew the truth of the proverb, "Custom rules the
law," and indeed the history of fairs may be taken as one
long commentary on this truth.

For all that, the riddle of which came first, the fair or the
festival, may be as insoluble as that of the hen and the egg.
We know that many of our ancient fairs are held on the local
patronal festival; but it does not necessarily follow that even
with these the fair did not predate the church. It is, in fact,
much more probable that when the church was built, in
keeping with Gregory's advice it was given the patronage of the
saint whose festival fell nearest to the time of the local fair.

And how well the tradition of burnt offerings has been

[1] Bede's *Ecclesiastical History*, book i, c. 30.

6

maintained! It seems odd to reflect that the custom of roasting the ox in the market place goes back through Christian sacrifice to those pagan ceremonies at the hero's grave. Indeed, it may not be straining the tradition to suggest that the butchers of Wigton in Cumberland who still hung carcases on their church doors in the seventeenth century, to be cut up into Sunday joints for sober parishioners after Mattins, were not only maintaining the custom of their ancestors who killed cattle "to the praise of God in their eating," but at the same time anticipating their Victorian descendants who observed it in the awful solemnities of the Sunday dinner. It is no more fanciful to believe this, surely, than to believe that the shops which encircle the churchyard in so many of our country towns are the direct successors of the first huts of green boughs set up to provide refreshment for those who came to make such sacrifices, as they commonly are.

The association of fairs with the shrines of Christian saints was preserved for centuries by holding them in churchyards, a custom which, although made illegal in 1285, continued in vigour at least until Henry VI's reign, when it became illegal to hold fairs on Ascension Day, Corpus Christi, Whit-Sunday, Trinity Sunday, the Assumption of the Virgin Mary, All Saints, Good Friday, or any Sunday, the four in harvest excepted. Any merchant who continued to sell after the termination of the fair, as fixed by the charter, was liable to forfeit to the king double the value of all that he sold.[1] But old customs die hard, and we find orders issued in Elizabeth I's reign enjoining "that in all fairs and common markets, falling upon the Sunday, there be no shewing of any wares before the service be done."

Time and place are, in fact, the two primary conditions of fairs. Huvelin goes so far as to say they are fixed so definitely that they must be accounted their fundamental characteristics, and, with the single exception of St. Ives, history no less than law may be held to confirm the view. We certainly find that, however slight the written evidence may be, clues to the antiquity of fairs by prescription are often to be found in their timing and siting.

The most considerable research into this part of the subject

[1] 2nd Edward III, c. 15, and 5th Edward III, c. 5.

7

was done by John Griffith, who in "The May or Gorsedd Year in English and Welsh Fairs," [1] shows that the overwhelming majority of fairs are not regulated by the solstitial year, with its quarter days on the 21st March, 21st June, 23rd September, and 23rd December, but by the older May or Gorsedd year, with its quarter days—astronomically indicated by alignments of megalithic monuments—falling on the 4th February, 6th May, 8th August, and 8th November. Taking Owen's *Book of Fairs* as the basis of his analysis he found that there were twice as many fairs in May as in June. He calculated, in fact, "that we have still in England and Wales two thousand three hundred and sixty-three relics of festivals held at the same spots or thereabouts when the dates were obtained by direct solar observations by means of aligned monuments." His argument is impressive, and no doubt his main contention is sound; but it has to be borne in mind that the dating of fairs was always related to the working seasons of the year as well as to religious or pagan festivals, and consequently spring and autumn were the most popular times. Perhaps, however, the distinction between Christian and pagan is unreal, because the great pagan festivals were obviously placed between the heavier labours of the year, when the people could spare time for recreation, and Christian festivals were, we may assume, accommodated to this settled practice. It is also probable that the many autumn fairs were made occasions of thanksgiving for the safe ingathering of crops in both pagan and Christian times.

The siting of ancient fairs is equally impressive. Many, as we should expect in view of Sir Henry Maine's observations on their origins, are held near boundaries and are still occasions of inter-parochial rivalry though with less violence than formerly. The fair at Purton, Wiltshire, [2] for example, used to end on the first day with a few sturdy fights, to be followed on the second with the champions of Purton challenging the champions of Stretton to compete with them at single-stick for such prizes as a new smock or a new hat. They were concerned, no doubt, to acquit themselves well in front of their sweethearts; but they contended primarily on behalf of their

---

[1] *Nature*, 5th September, 1907.
[2] E. M. Richardson, *The Story of Purton*.

respective villages rather than for personal honour—as, of course, we do still in our weekly cricket matches. Such rivalry has always been common everywhere, and is obviously a peaceful and friendly survival of the almost continuous warfare there was between neighbouring tribes when fairs were first established.

The other and perhaps more popular site was the hill top. Hardy's "Greenhill" was no exception. And these hill-top fairs are particularly interesting because they are frequently found at points where ancient trackways, or green roads, intersect, and not infrequently near funeral barrows. We shall have several to discuss when we come to examine the distribution of fairs regionally. The most famous of all was that on St. Giles's Hill at Winchester, which had a Long Barrow near. Another familiar example is that at Tan Hill, near Devizes in Wiltshire, held on St. Lawrence's Day on a hill which would form a meeting place for merchants and chapmen travelling along well-trodden prehistoric trackways. Dr. Dexter believed that this particular fair goes back to the Bronze Age. Wiltshire has several such fairs. Another held annually at an earthwork is that at Yarnborough Castle, Hanging Langford. Other hill-top fairs in the same region are those at Martinsell Hill near Marlborough, Silbury near Avebury, and Bidcombe near Warminster.

In the north of England, where Scandinavian influence was strong, the link between fairs and prehistoric sites of assembly may be traced in such names as Tingley, near Wakefield. Tingley is a corruption of *Thinglawe*, or assembly-hill, and it stands at the intersection of the two ancient trackways that to-day link Wakefield with Bradford and Dewsbury with Leeds. Nearby is held Lee Gap Fair, perhaps the oldest horse fair in Yorkshire.

In considering these associations of fairs with prehistoric trackways it is, however, necessary to keep in mind that the action would be reciprocal—that is to say, as the trackways gave rise to the fairs through caravans of traders meeting each other where their routes crossed, so the fairs would affect the popularity of the tracks, increasing the traffic on the most convenient and reducing that on others, until the pilgrim tracks of one age became the trade routes of the next.

So while we may not have records of such merchants and merchandise as we find in Ezekiel, the old green roads of England can fill the imagination with visions of English shepherds driving their flocks to the great sheep fairs of Wessex, or of Scots and Welsh shepherds bringing them south and east to the fairs of Northumberland in the north, and of Shropshire pre-eminently in the west, many of which have flourished from time immemorial.

But fascinating as the pre-history of fairs may be, much must remain speculative until we come to the granting of charters. It is with these that their authentic history begins. By developing the trade and communications of the country the Romans, who are credited by Cornelius Walford [1] with having introduced fairs into England, would do much to promote them; but most of what the Romans did must remain obscure because so many of their fairs fell away after the Roman withdrawal, with the result that references to fairs and markets in Domesday are negligible. This, however, shows only that, when the Normans came, they were not of much value as sources of revenue. But this was soon altered. In the twelfth and thirteenth centuries practically all our historic English fairs became chartered and were reconstituted, more or less to conform with the flourishing fairs on the Continent. Troy weight, which we use to this day, takes its name from Troyes Fair in France. Similarly, some of our present-day banking devices originated in the system devised for the fairs of Champagne. By this introduction of French methods the old English fairs rapidly became sources of great and increasing wealth; their tolls, coveted possessions. But it must never be forgotten that many of the fairs at which the right to receive tolls was granted by the Normans—in return for their control and organization—had existed time out of mind.

But while the granting of charters was in effect the granting of revenues from fairs rather than of the right to establish fairs, the right of toll was not incident to a fair. It had to be specifically mentioned in the charter. The owner could not be allowed complete freedom in this, otherwise he might have strangled trade by his greed. As a safeguard against this particular danger exemption from toll was regularly granted

[1] *Fairs Past and Present.*

10

to the merchants upon whom the initial prosperity of fairs depended. Indeed in several towns, specially privileged because staple commodities were produced in them, this valuable exemption would be given to the burgesses as a body and might extend to all fairs and markets throughout the kingdom. Similar privileges were granted to merchants from overseas. Henry II granted to the merchants of Cologne visiting the London fairs protection identical with that enjoyed by his own subjects.

Outside the counties palatine, the sovereign alone had power to grant fairs, and in early times he invariably granted them either to a nobleman in reward for services rendered in time of war, or to a religious house as a form of endowment. In his survey of the Somerset fairs, Dr. Hulbert draws attention to the granting of half a dozen fairs in 1304 and of several others soon afterwards, which we may safely assume were rewards for services to the king in the Scottish wars. Indeed one charter expressly refers to the grantee as having been "in service with the king in Scotland." As an example of the other kind of grantee, Dr. Hulbert cites a fair given to the monks of Cleeve Abbey to enable them to meet a large capital outlay, to which they were committed as the result of a calamity that had befallen them. Similar grants were made to both the great feudal families and the many religious houses of the north. The Percies, for example, were granted fairs at Ilkley, Kildale, Carnaby, Pocklington, Pannal and Wansford, Topcliffe-upon-Swale, Seamer, and Leckonfield. The Nevilles had fairs at Pickhill, Sheriff Hutton and Middleham; the Scropes at Croft, Burton Constable, Masham, and so on. No doubt national calamities were followed as a matter of course by the widespread granting of charters, and one of the most profitable lines of inquiry that might be undertaken into this still largely uncharted subject would be to set out the dates of fair charters county by county in relation to war, pestilence, and other visitations, particularly in relation to the Black Death in the middle of the fourteenth century.

But while the right to exact toll was not incident to the granting of a fair, the right to hold a court of piepowder was. This curious name is a corruption of the Old French for pedlar —*pied pouldre*. It was the court of the dusty-footed, that is

11

to say, of the wandering chapmen who frequented fairs and required an immediate settlement of their disputes at each before moving on to the next. Formalities were reduced to the minimum. The answer to a summons might be required within an hour, and at most within a day.

The only direct references to these courts of piepowder in Acts of Parliament are in the statutes of 17 Edward IV, c. 2 and 1 Richard III, c. 6, in the earlier of which it is stated to be a presumption of law that to every fair "there is of right pertaining a court of Pypowders, to minister in the same due justice on his behalf; in which court every person coming to the said fair should have lawful remedy of all manner of contracts, trespasses, covenants, debts, and other deeds made or done within the jurisdiction of the same, and to be tried by merchants being of the same fair." As the name implies, this court of piepowder, of which records are common from Henry III's reign onwards, was introduced by the Normans when they reconstituted the old English fairs; but with the courts no less than with the fairs themselves it was a re-organization of something already in existence. At Bristol and Gloucester, courts of piepowder sat in connection with the Tolzey court, which dates from Saxon times. The name survives in Tolbooth. What happened at Bristol was that from the 29th of September the court of piepowder sat for fourteen days before a steward of the Tolzey court, which was suspended for that period, and at the end of these fourteen days the proceedings were adjourned into the Tolzey. At Hemel Hempstead a court of piepowder was kept going until 1898 to deal with all matters relating to the local markets and market buildings. Eye in Suffolk has a Piepowder Court Book for the period 1732–1813, with carefully written headings for each successive year without a break; but the sole entry in all that long period is under date 1737 and concerns no less a matter than the sale of "a black gelding with one eye" for 24*s*.! According to Gross's *Law Merchant*, sessions of such courts were held occasionally in several old boroughs in 1835, and at Bartholomew Fair, London, they were held regularly up to 1854.

By the earlier of the two charters just mentioned the jurisdiction of the court was restricted to what happened within the precinct of the fair and the term of its duration. Judgment, however, could be deferred until the next court. Notwithstanding this, however, the 1448 statute shows that abuses had crept in, and that courts of piepowder had become money-making institutions assuming authority to which they had no right. Apparently it was extremely difficult to control them because the authority in the various courts in any particular region was usually in the same hands. So if the person presiding at a court of piepowder lacked authority in one capacity he probably possessed it in another. To himself, therefore, and to the majority of those who appeared before him, it was immaterial in which capacity he was acting at any given moment. In those circumstances it is not surprising that we should find several vivacious accounts of such courts in literature—most amusingly, perhaps, in Ben Jonson's *Bartholomew Fair*, presided over by Justice Overdo.

But there were notable exceptions to this combined authority. Originally, when fair charters were being granted exclusively to noblemen, the court of piepowder was invariably held before the lord of the manor's steward, who did, of course, preside over other courts. But in course of time practically all the old fairs came into the hands of the Church. With these the abbot or bishop might have jurisdiction in the court of piepowder only. Nevertheless, if he happened to be the largest landowner in the district we find that while the court of piepowder sat, all other authority in the locality was suspended—that is to say, the municipal officials were required to hand over the entire control of the town to the charter-owning clerics for the duration of the fair. After the dissolution of the monasteries the court of piepowder in corporate towns was usually presided over by the mayor or his deputy and two citizens; and here again the mayor had dual authority because he was chairman of the local bench of magistrates. Finally, the County Courts Act of 1888 enabled the lord of the manor, or any other fair owner, to surrender the right of holding such courts to the Crown, and at this date most of them lapsed.

But long before this time fairs had ceased to be vital to the nation's economy, so their control was no longer of prime importance. The scene at the usual fair of the post-Reformation period is graphically delineated by Gay in his character of the ballad singer in *The Shepherd's Week*, where he presents the stalls, the lotteries, the mountebanks, the tumblers, the rope-dancers, the raree-shows, the puppets, and "all the fun o' the fair."

> How pedlars' stalls with glittering toys are laid,
> The various fairings of the country maid:
> Long silken laces hang upon the twine,
> And rows of pins and amber bracelets shine;
> How the tight lass knives, combs, and scissors spies,
> And looks on thimbles with desiring eyes.
> Of lotteries next with tuneful note he told,
> Where silver spoons are won, and rings of gold:
> The lads and lasses trudge the streets along,
> And all the fair is crowded in his song.
> The mountebank now treads the stage, and sells
> His pills, his balsams, and his ague-spells;
> Now o'er and o'er the nimble tumbler springs,
> And on the rope the venturous maiden swings;
> Jack Pudding, in his party-coloured jacket,
> Tosses the glove, and jokes at every packet.
> Of raree-shows he sung, and Punch's feats,
> Of pockets picked in crowds, and various cheats.

What a tangled skein it is! Yet every thread has its own significant suggestion of an exciting origin. It was to present the Creation as a mystery play that the first Wild Beast Shows were brought together, and our paltry fairings go back through representations of popular saints in gingerbread to the relics which are the clue to the rise of the greatest of all our fairs, because while the origins of fairs as an institution followed the lines already traced, the success of the greatest was due in the first place to the renown of miracle-working relics which made the churches that held them places of pilgrimage. Even the pious must adjourn their worship to eat, and at festivals of popular saints booths were set up for refreshments, followed directly by the stalls of merchants and mountebanks of every description, who seized the opportunities provided by these huge assemblies, until festivals became fairs and fairs became marts. And as the Church created the

14

conditions she was quick to collect the profits. Thus hundreds of charters were granted to clerics in the thirteenth and fourteenth centuries by devout or nervous sovereigns for the good of their souls, or the repose of the souls of their ancestors, and for a while no one was the poorer.

## CHAPTER II

# Fairs and the Church

To trace the development of fairs in general stage by stage is impossible, because few of them were free to develop in a normal organic manner. In any case, adequate records are lacking. The fairs with the most reliably documented history are those that were owned by dignitaries of the Church, who alone exploited them fully and raised them to their greatest prosperity, even if, by their arrogance and greed, they were also responsible for much of the ultimate failure. And with those of the Bible before them it is hardly surprising that these abbots and bishops should have been so ambitious in planning their fairs. It was to the East that everyone looked in the Middle Ages when indulging in high-flown covetous dreams:

> In Syria whilom dwelt a company
> Of chapmen rich, and thereto sad and true
> That widëwherë sent their spicery,
> Clothës of gold, and satins rich of hue.
> Their chaffare was so thrifty and so new,
> That every wight had dainty to chaffare
> With them, and eke to sellë them their ware.[1]

[1] Chaucer, *The Man of Lawe's Tale.*

18

## Biblical Evidence

Every learned man knew something of the trade routes of Asia, of the caravans and ships that bore the costly merchandise of the cities of Mesopotamia and Arabia, of the world of Solomon and Sheba. He knew from Ezekiel of the fairs of "Tyre, the crowning city, whose merchants are princes, whose traffickers are the honourable of the earth." He had read of Joseph being brought from a pit and sold to the Ishmaelites, who "came from Gilead, with their camels bearing spicery and balm and myrrh," and who apparently knew all there is to be known about monopolies and the cornering of markets, for great as several of our English fairs became, they were never really to be compared with those of the East. Think, for instance, of Richard Cœur de Lion capturing one of Saladin's caravans in the Third Crusade and gaining thereby "very rich spoil of spices, gold, silver, silks, robes, arms of every kind, together with four thousand seven hundred camels, besides asses and mules without number."

But if English fairs were never renowned for the costliest merchandise—"emeralds, purple, and broidered work, and fine linen and coral and agate," yet "with silver, iron, tin, and lead they traded . . . with horses . . . lambs and rams and goats." And even English trade had a romance in the Middle Ages which can only be imagined to-day by creating anew the whole environment of mediæval life. As iron, for example, which the Industrial Revolution turned into the symbol of all that is dull and insensitive, was "bright iron" —a precious metal—in Ezekiel, so it was to the lord of a mediæval English manor, who sent his bailiff to buy it in bars at the great fairs of Sturbridge, Winchester, Boston, and St. Ives. And there was wealth as well as romance. The grievance was that so much of it found its way into the coffers of the Church, and so little was left to the traders.

It is true, of course, that the Church had much to contribute to fairs as well as much to derive from them. Wool, cloth, and hides were their staple commodities, and these had their principal source in the flocks and herds of the abbots, even though no one knew better than the abbot that the secret of his initial success was not in the value of the commodities he offered for sale, but in the superstitious regard of the people for the relics preserved in his church. The commercial

19

success was secondary. But what an opportunity a festival provided! His religious duties discharged, the abbot had no compunction in making temporal provision for the community he ruled, and for the work of charity entrusted to him, by turning these assemblies of the faithful into marts for the disposal of wool and cloth and any other surplus products of the abbey. He was only doing what had been done for centuries. The very name, 'fair' is derived from *feria*, or festival. Not only did the priests of Jupiter invest large sums of money with the merchants who frequented their fairs, but in Christian times a fair had been held annually from time immemorial at the most sacred place of all, Mount Calvary.

The exploitation of fairs by the English Church began in the time of Henry I, who in his long reign of thirty-five years granted charters to many—probably most—of the greater churches. To Canterbury he granted one to be held on the Feast of St. Augustine's Translation, and after the canonization of St. Thomas à Becket, followed by the report that miracles had been worked both at his grave and at the well where his garments had been washed, so many pilgrims flocked to this particular shrine that not only did Canterbury flourish, but the dates of fairs in other towns were altered to catch pilgrims either going or coming. Guildford Fair, for instance, was moved from Christmas to September with this in view. The great fair at Shalford nearby similarly owed its prosperity to the patronage of Canterbury Pilgrims. Among others of the greater churches to receive fairs, St. Andrew's Priory at Rochester received the grant of "all customs and liberties and the entire toll of the two days fair on the Feast of St. Paulinus, whose body rests in the church of St. Andrew the Apostle in the same city" [1]; St. Albans Abbey in Hertfordshire, one of eight days at the Nativity of St. John the Baptist; and St. Peter's at Bath, the grant of a fair in "alms and augmentation of the Episcopal see" on its patronal festival, "so that the bishop may have his seat there with the greatest honour." The list might be continued to cover the entire kingdom. So important were fairs in the Middle Ages that at least three that were granted to the greater churches—those at St. Albans, Peterborough, and Bury St.

[1] Report of Royal Commission, 1889.

20

Edmunds—were the means by which the Church, and the Church alone, produced the town.

In spite of the rivalry thus created, the saint with the greatest drawing power in southern England continued to be St. Thomas à Becket. Most of the fairs held on or near the date of his translation were associated with him. Many of them, in fact, were known quite simply as Becket Fairs. The fair at Bromeshill, near Brandon Ferry, and that at West Acre near Swaffham, were two of them. But popular as St. Thomas was everywhere, the most venerated saints in East Anglia were St. Edmund, whose fair is chiefly remembered now as an elegant social occasion and will be discussed later, and St. Etheldreda, daughter of Anna, king of the East Angles, who in 673 founded a religious community in the Fens at Ely and became its first abbess.

For more than 400 years Etheldreda's foundation had a chequered existence. Its eventual prosperity began in October, 1106, with the translation of her remains to the new church, which less than three years later became the cathedral church of a new diocese. Thus Ely became a place of pilgrimage, and with all the conditions for a prosperous fair established, the bishop obtained from the king—again Henry I—a charter for a fair to be held on the anniversary of Etheldreda's death and the three days before and after it. And so popular, incidentally, did this fair in the Fens become that it gave a new word to the language. In the *Liber Eliensis* it is related that St. Etheldreda, who was known to the people as St. Audrey, pleaded so powerfully on behalf of a penitent thief that his chains were struck off and he was restored to freedom. In gratitude he became a monk of Ely, hanging his broken chains in the abbey church as testimony. These chains were reproduced in lace called "St. Audrey's chains," which were sold as a fairing at Ely at least until 1913. In course of time their name, St. Audrey, was corrupted to tawdry and extended to include any and every kind of cheap or pretentious adornment. Originally it was confined to St. Audrey's lace.

Another incidental feature at Ely was an attempt to rid the fair of rogues and vagabonds by incorporating in the proclamation a command that "all vagabonds, idle and misbehaving persons, all cheaters, cozeners, rogues, sturdy

21

beggars and shifters do depart out of this fair immediately
after this proclamation of the bishop, upon pain of imprison-
ment and further correction by the Court in the fair, that is
to say, the Court of Piepowder, that his Majesty's good subjects may be the more quiet, and that the king's peace may
be the better upheld." This threat, needless to say, had no
legal warrant whatever, since the court of piepowder had no
jurisdiction over what happened outside the precincts of the
fair and the period covered by its charter.

Later in its history Ely had two fairs, the original one on
the anniversary of Etheldreda's death and a second on the
anniversary of her translation; but both—like most of the
other forty-four fairs of Cambridgeshire and the Isle of Ely—
have fallen away and are now so insignificant that they bear
no resemblance to the great fair referred to by Matthew
Paris and Camden. No longer is a fenland Autolycus to be
heard crying St. Audrey's wares:

> Lawn as white as driven snow;
> Cyprus black as e'er was crow;
> Gloves as sweet as damask roses;
> Masks for faces and for noses;
> Bugle-bracelet, necklace-amber,
> Perfume for a lady's chamber;
> Golden quoifs and stomachers,
> For my lads to give their dears;
> Pins and poking-sticks of steel;
> What maids lack from head to heel.

Many other cathedral cities grew rich on these fairs
granted by Henry I—Exeter, Chester, Hereford, Ripon, and
so on—and we usually find their fortunes begin to rise with
the introduction of relics. Perhaps the most remarkable
example of this is St. Ives, which will be considered in the
next chapter. Its charter was granted in 1110, but the fair was
undoubtedly the result of relics alleged to have been found
there in 1002. In the north of England, St. Etheldreda at Ely
could be matched on a smaller scale by St. Hilda at Whitby;
but the only northern prelates who owned fairs on a princely
scale were the archbishops of York and the bishops of Durham.

The three greatest fairs belonging to the archbishop of
York were those of York, Ripon, and Beverley, in all of

which the Church's authority—not to say avarice—was stoutly resisted, particularly in the fourteenth and fifteenth centuries. By this time the citizens themselves had obtained charters to hold fairs in most of the important towns, and in consequence they had come to regard the Church's privileges at fairs as obsolete. The most determined clash was at Ripon, where a fair had been granted to the archbishop and St. Wilfrid by Henry I in 1108. The archbishop of York, while acknowledging the rights of citizens in their own fairs, as he was bound to do, had always been wily enough to see that these did not interfere with his. By the beginning of the fifteenth century the people of Ripon had come to feel that the episcopal yoke should be removed, and a resistance movement was started, led by the king's tenants in the forest of Knaresborough, who no doubt regarded themselves as a privileged class. This movement came to a head in 1441, when the Knaresborough men refused to pay toll to the archbishop of York for the right to sell their wares in what they felt was their own market town, upon which the primate, too proud to submit his claims to law, hired 200 men-at-arms from Scotland and the Marches to enforce them. This was too much for the Yorkshire dalesmen, and 700 of them, led by Sir John Plumpton, marched into Ripon by night and turned the fairground into a battlefield.

No better proof of the value of these fairs to the dignitaries of the Church could be found than the tenacity with which they clung to them. Many towns were held in a grip that amounted to a stranglehold. Reading was ruled by its abbots for 250 years. They owned the mills and fisheries along its streams, as well as its fairs and markets. Indeed its entire trade was in their hands. In the Midlands there were complaints from the citizens of Lichfield, and 17 miles northwest of Lichfield the strained relationship between Church and people was to be seen again at Stafford, where the friars claimed the king's protection from common hucksters, complaining that at local fairs and markets they were prevented from buying their victuals, and that even when they succeeded, the goods they bought were snatched from their hands. Moving to the east of England we find even more violent scenes at Bury St. Edmunds, where the abbey was despoiled by an angry mob, who killed the prior as a demonstration against the tyranny of the Church.

If the abbot was not too high and mighty, a compromise might be agreed upon, as it was, apparently, at Chester, where the abbot conciliated the burgesses in various ways during the prolonged struggle between them, amusing them with mystery plays and similar entertainments, which, although they had been an integral part of festivals long before enmity developed between Church and people, were used at this time as a sop. Finally, when the abbot saw that he was beaten, he conceded to the citizens most of the trading privileges they claimed, even allowing them the right of "stallage" throughout the city in return for an annual payment of 46s. 8d. At Norwich the bailiffs of the prior and convent of Holy Trinity met the bailiffs of the city before the fair and divided up the ground into four equal parts. One half of each of these quarters was allowed to the citizens quit of toll on condition they chose their sites on Friday the morrow of the Ascension, and occupied them before sunset on the following Tuesday. This Norwich fair, known later as Tombland Fair, because held in an open space near the cathedral, developed undoubtedly from the booths set up to provide refreshments for pilgrims who came to pay their devotions at the end of Holy Week.

The greatest indignity to which the civic authorities were subjected at so many of the greater fairs was the obligation to relinquish all authority to the owner of the franchise for the duration of the fair. The most far-reaching instance of this was at Winchester, and will be described presently; but the same happened elsewhere. When at York the bell rang at 3 p.m. on Old Lammas Day, the sheriffs handed their white rods of office, the symbols of their authority, to the archbishop's representatives, who immediately took over the entire control of the city, even empanelling for the court of piepowder a jury drawn exclusively from Wistow, a township within the archbishop's liberty. At Hereford, where originally a like surrender of power was demanded, the bishops, like those of Chester, had the good sense to come to terms with the town. It might, perhaps, be argued that at Hereford there was justification for a temporary assumption of authority by

24

the Church, because there nearly half the city, as well as a substantial part of the suburbs, formed the bishop's fee, a district of special privilege in which the bishop always had enjoyed rights of *infangenethef* and *utfangenethef*,[1] which meant that he had in his hands the administration of the law, and the charge of prisoners by his own appointed officers in the episcopal gaol, which was, in fact, inside the palace. For centuries these rights extended to the entire city for the period of the fair; but by 1557, at all events, the original demands had been modified, because we find that Walter Carwardine, who was mayor that year, admitted "the bishop's right to hold a court in his palace for the settlement of all actions and disputes arising during the fair, and that all fines for trespass or affrays then committed, and two parts of the tolls paid by strangers resorting at that time to the city, were due to the bishop, but declared that the remaining third, with all fines for bloodshed, belonged to the mayor, and should be paid to him for the benefit of the city; and that the mayors from time immemorial, every year at the end of the fair, had been accustomed after court time, personally or by their officers, to make a proclamation at the bishop's palace gate, commanding his bailiff to cease holding the fair, and to send any complaints remaining unsettled to the city courts on the morrow, when all apprehended felons were delivered over to the mayor."

St. Ethelbert's Fair at Hereford, for which a charter was granted by Henry I in 1117 or thereabouts, began on the 19th May and was originally for the usual three days only— the vigil, feast, and morrow of the saint. In course of time, however, it was prolonged to nine days, and again was the outstanding event in the city year. On the morning of the 19th the bishop's bailiff, accompanied by the steward, rode to the palace and summoned by name all the bishop's tenants, calling upon them to attend him about the city while he proclaimed the fair. Sometimes as many as 200 would respond, and these would follow the bailiff as—with the mace carried before him—he rode to the city gates, halting at each to appoint three porters, who, after being duly sworn were charged to collect tolls of all who entered while the fair was

---

[1] From the Saxon *fang*, to take, and *thef* or *theof*, a thief.

in progress.[1] This done, the bailiff and his attendants rode to the High Cross, where the fair was solemnly proclaimed by the city crier.

On the completion of the proclamation ceremony the bailiff became chief magistrate, and went in procession to the palace, there to hold his first court, while the sergeant-at-mace went out to collect tolls from the stall-holders. Pitching-pence, and the proceeds from all stands erected on the high causeway were the bailiff's perquisites. After the bailiff had administered the oath to the jury and other officers of the fair, including the leather-searchers and ale-tasters, he would himself go the rounds of the fair, stopping, perhaps, to taste samples of butter, which he might seize in bulk if he thought them bad. Usually, no doubt, he was a just man. The office had come to him by election and not by arbitrary appointment. But authority might go to his head occasionally, as it did, presumably, with the bailiff who clapped a poor ballad singer in gaol for singing without his leave.

As elsewhere, disputes were frequent between the city and the palace, and the right was not always on the people's side. As early as 1240 the bishop complained against certain of the citizens for selling wool, hides, and other goods privately in their own houses during fair time instead of openly in the fair, thus defrauding him of his dues. They admitted the offence, but argued that the bishop did not suffer if they informed the bailiff of their sales and paid what was due. The bishop, of course, replied that if this were permitted evasion would become easy, and in any case he would lose stallage.[2] But he can have had little to complain about. We get an idea of the bishop's profits from the fact that only one-tenth of his revenue from the fair was required to endow the chapel of St. Mary Magdalene, which stood south of the cathedral in what is now the bishop's garden.

These exactions were obviously a drain on the commercial resources of the city, and it is not surprising that so many records connected with the people's grievances should be

---

[1] The porters at Hereford are referred to in the records as *Insidiatores*. They were paid 6*d.* a day, which was four times the rate paid to labourers working at the wall.

[2] *Curia Regis*, 121, m. 29.

preserved in the cathedral archives. For all that, the bishop's fair at Hereford survived the Dissolution, and even the Commonwealth. But here again we find a second fair being granted, and this to the citizens, to whom Henry III granted one to be held at the feast of St. Denis. But although the bishop's fair would be undermined by the people's, its final decline as a source of revenue would be due to the setting up of regular weekly markets. Finally, at the beginning of Queen Victoria's reign,[1] the duration of St. Ethelbert's fair was reduced to two days, and the court of piepowder, with all rights to appoint officers to superintend pickage, stallage, foldage, and so forth, was transferred to the Corporation, along with all the emoluments and dues of the fair. The bishop's profits, which for a long time had amounted to very little, were commuted for twelve and a half bushels of best wheat, or the value thereof, to be paid to the bishop annually. So the bishop's tenants at Hampton Bishop were no longer required to cut six loads of wattles from the Haywood and bring them into the city for the construction of booths, and eventually all the ceremonies connected with the fair were abandoned. It now survives as an annual jollification for the young, and an annual nuisance for everyone else. It is held on the first Wednesday in May, and for three days civic life is completely disorganized. In the early hours of Tuesday morning the showmen move in and the streets are crammed with all the trappings and paraphernalia of carnival. Traffic has to be diverted, bus routes altered, and such are the difficulties of policing the city that everyone wonders how much longer the Chief Constable will tolerate this fair in the streets; others, however, may value it as a reminder of the great fair of St. Ethelbert, which once contributed so much to the prosperity of Hereford and the wealth of the see. Others again have a sentimental regard for it as having inspired some vivid scenes in the poems of Hereford's poet laureate, John Masefield.

Few of the larger cities would permit such fairs to-day. Once they lose their commercial function decadence sets in, and it was for this reason that so many were suppressed towards the end of the nineteenth century. But again, it is easy

[1] 1 & 2 Victoria, c. 69.

to exaggerate the increase in depravity. The scenes at many of the London fairs before they were abolished were in every way intolerable; but they may have been no worse than those in every cathedral city, now so prim and respectable, at the end of the Middle Ages, when the Church had grown lax. Bunyan's "Vanity Fair," set up by Beelzebub, Apollyon and Legion in the town of Vanity may be less fanciful than we suppose. What aggravates the offence is that these festival fairs were held, as the name implies, on holy days. Thus the patronal festival of the Church, a day of solemn dedication, was the busiest, rowdiest day of the year, the one on which there was the least opportunity for worship. No wonder the statute of 1448 ran: "Considering the abominable injuries and offences done to Almighty God and His saints, always aiders and singular assisters in our necessities, because of fairs and markets upon their high and principal feasts . . . as though they [the people] did no way remember the horrible defiling of their souls in the buying and selling, with many deceitful lies and false perjury, with drunkenness and strifes, and so withdrawing themselves and their servants from divine service."

In view of the disorderliness of fairs in the later Middle Ages it is hardly surprising that the connection between these and the Church should have been severed at the Reformation. Up to then the great abbeys continued to control, though with weakening hands, the commercial as well as the religious life of the towns in which they were situated, although it ought to be said that the actual conduct of the trading interests was usually entrusted to lay brothers. As for the other connection, that between religion and merrymaking, the Puritans tried to break this in the next century, when so innocent a fairing as a basket of gingerbread was denounced as "a basket of popery, a nest of images, and whole legend of ginger-work." Happily the earlier movement succeeded, the later one failed, although it must be admitted that these annual bouts of dissipation may have caused a good deal of poverty both before and after. "Every town, parish, and village," says Stubbs in his *Anatomie of Abuses*, "some at one time of the year, some at another (but so that everyone keeps his proper day assigned and appropriate to itself which they call their wake-

28

day), useth to make great preparation and provision for good
cheer, to which their friends and kinsfolks far and near are
invited, insomuch as the poor men that bear the charges
of these feasts keep the worse houses a long time after."
When fairs had first been granted, their proper control had
always been an important stipulation. It was for this reason
that they had been granted to nobles. But when these nobles
had themselves become a menace they had been granted to
clerics, who were thought less likely to make them occasions
of insurrection. Who can doubt, for example, that the revolt
of the barons did more than his own piety to influence King
John in granting fairs so generously to the Church. But with
the Church's decadence security at fairs—economic and
political—was again lost, with the difference that the peasants
rather than the barons were now to be feared, particularly
after the revolt of 1381. So we may say, that as the easy
wealth that came to the Church through her fairs contributed
much to her decay, so in turn the Church's laxity contributed
to the decay of fairs. Moreover, with increasing weakness she
became incapable of adapting her rule to altered social conditions, and trade was crippled and stunted by restrictive
regulation and taxation that left nothing for enterprise and
development.

Thus it was that mediæval fairs and the mediæval Church
in England waxed and waned together, although the fairs,
as secondary, declined more rapidly than the Church. Their
period of greatest prosperity was between 1200 and 1400. In
those two centuries no fewer than 4,860 were granted—3,300
in the thirteenth century, 1,560 in the fourteenth. After that
they declined so abruptly that only 100 were granted in the
fifteenth century. By this time, of course, the country must
have been practically covered by the earlier grants, and as the
number increased their dating had to be arranged to safeguard those already established.

There were other considerations. These thousands of fairs
meant that there was always a large mobile population in
the country, which had to be fed and quartered. In the Middle
Ages the Church, and the Church alone, could organize this.
Again, the greater fairs, and some of the smaller ones, had to
be arranged so that merchants could move from one to

another in a regular sequence. Nor were transport and hospitality the only problems. The merchants wanted to buy as well as sell, and it was necessary for them to visit fairs at times when the goods they needed were available. This regular circuit is reflected in letters patent of the 14th November, 1240, in which the bailiffs of Winchester were ordered to make known to all merchants "the provision of the King and Council that the King's prises [1] from merchants shall be paid at four terms of the year, to wit, prises due at the fair of Northampton in the fair of St. Ives; prises due in the latter, at the fair of Boston; prises in the latter, in the fair of Winchester, and those due in the latter in the fair of Northampton." Other fairs, of course, were attended between. The merchants who attended Boston Fair, for example, would go from there to a fair at King's Lynn. So there was obviously a limit to the number of fairs possible, and continuing need for such services as only the Church had so far been able to provide. The breaking away of commerce was, therefore, by no means a simple process, and there long remained both a credit and a debit side to the Church's account with fairs. In particular it is to be remembered that however obstructive the Church had become towards the end of the Middle Ages, there had been her fostering care at the beginning. It was with commerce then as it is with education in our own time. The parent Church was trying to cling to the child after it had outgrown her control. Causes for complaint were substantial enough; but the high-handed action of the archbishops of York, and of so many other dignitaries of the Church, does not invalidate the benefits that accrued from the foundations of commerce laid by the abbots and bishops to whom fairs had been granted in the twelfth and thirteenth centuries, in particular the benefits the whole nation derived from the great Cistercian abbeys' fostering of the wool trade —the wool, on which, as we are so often reminded, the nation's wealth is founded. The abbots, whose flocks were fattened on the plains and marshland pastures of East Anglia, on the moors and downs of the West Country, and on the fells of the north, were its great producers. And as for their control, which

[1] 'Prise' was obligatory at any price the King's agents were pleased to name.

society outgrew, it had in the first place been the substitution for the armed protection of feudal lords, of the blessing and fatherly care of the Christian faith—not unmingled, it is true, with its threats and penances. If the people of Ripon had reason to fear the predominance of the Church, those of other places—of Hedon, near Beverley, for example, which became an important township in the Middle Ages as the result of its association with the hospital of St. Mary Magdalen—had cause to be grateful for it. Magdalen Fair at Hedon, granted to the brethren of the Hospital by Henry II, which continued until the nineteenth century, was one of the most popular in in the north, and similar instances could be found in every part of the kingdom.

# CHAPTER III

# The Four Great Fairs of England

*Winchester – St. Ives – Sturbridge – St. Bartholomew*

Not everyone, perhaps, would agree that the fairs of Winchester, St. Ives, Sturbridge, and St. Bartholomew are correctly described as the four great fairs of England. What of Boston and Northampton fairs, which were probably of equal rank with those of Winchester and St. Ives during John's reign? That St. Bartholomew's was the greatest of all the London fairs, and Sturbridge the greatest of all the English fairs, is beyond dispute. These have no rivals. The others had varying fortunes, and if sufficient records were available, which they are not, the most useful way to study them would be to couple Winchester and Boston, the two comparable fairs with easy access to the sea, and St. Ives and Northampton, which were in rivalry for inland trade, although both had, in fact, international importance. The records being what they are, however, Northampton and Boston fairs cannot now be adequately presented as examples of great English fairs in their prime, while the others can;

but we do not forget that the husting of London was suspended during Boston Fair as well as during Winchester, which is sufficient indication of its eminence. We know, however, that Boston declined before Winchester, because in 1416 it was submitted that "the holding of the fair had entirely ceased for many years, and that there was therefore no excuse for interrupting the usual course of legal business in London." [1] Of the other pair, the fair at St. Ives has the advantage of having been the subject of detailed examination by historians of such eminence as Gross and Maitland.

## I.—WINCHESTER

Of these four great fairs of England Winchester has the earliest charter, while its hill-top site near a Long Barrow denotes an antiquity that can hardly be calculated. Situated as it is on a navigable river within easy reach of the sea, the natural advantages of St. Giles's Hill had always been apparent, and after the fair had been granted in 1094 to Bishop Walkelin by his kinsman William Rufus to assist the bishop in building his cathedral church, social advantages were added, which later were immeasurably enhanced by Winchester's status as a capital city ruled by such a prince of the Church as Pierre des Roches, at one time the most powerful man in the kingdom, under whom Winchester rivalled London as a mart. Its gilds grew rich on the cloth woven from the wool of the downland sheep, which was exchanged at the fair on St. Giles's Hill for iron from Spain, wine from Gascony, spices from the East, woad from Toulouse, as well as textiles, madder, and brassware from the Low Countries and the Rhineland, while its livestock was no less surprising and exotic. Apes, bears, and every species of vendible beast and bird was to be bought at Winchester Fair by those who had a fancy for outlandish creatures, as well as everything else that might pander to vanity and indulgence. "To Wy (Weyhill) and to Wynchestre," says Avarice in *Piers the Plowman*, "I went to the faire." And on such merchandise the bishop grew rich, because in no other fair had he such absolute authority over so large an area for so long a time.

[1] H. T. Riley, *Memorials of London and London Life*, p. 657.

Originally, St. Giles's Fair at Winchester was for the usual three days only—the vigil, feast, and morrow of the saint; but so prosperous did it become that the period was extended by Henry I, Stephen, Henry Plantagenet (who increased its duration to sixteen days), and Edward II, who in 1317 granted a charter for twenty-four days. Sixteen days, however, became the normal duration, and this we may be sure was long enough for the citizens of Winchester. The annual ceremony was similar to that already described at Hereford. On the vigil of the saint all who owed allegiance to the bishop were bound to assemble before 6 o'clock in the morning at the bishop's Court of Pavilion, which stood on St. Giles's Hill where "Palm Hall" was built later, and make their suit of service. Thereafter they were in duty bound to keep themselves in readiness with both horses and arms to answer the call if needed.

As at Hereford and other places, the city gates were sealed. The seneschal, attended either by a justice of the bishop's court, or the bishop's treasurer, rode into the city from Wolvesey Palace, entering at Kingsgate, where the party was awaited by the mayor and other representatives of municipal authority, prepared to make absolute surrender of their power, and to hand over the keys of the city gates, to which, the charter stated, "The Justiciaries shall at their own pleasure set their own warders or porters," who at Winchester were called "catch-poles." The city weighing machine, used by the Pesager in levying toll on imports, was then trundled up St. Giles's Hill for use by the bishop's officers.

Fairs were invariably opened with the reading of the proclamation, which did, however, vary in form and length both at different times and different places. At Winchester it was read at either Kingsgate or Southgate, whichever the justiciaries found most convenient. The next ceremony was the sitting of the court of the Soke,[1] here called the "Cheyne" court, at which the bishop's officers were sworn—the marshal, usher, chamberlain, coroner, and doubtless others. It was at this court also that the mayor and bailiffs were officially dismissed and others set up in their stead for the sixteen days of the fair.

[1] A Saxon word with the same meaning as Liberty.

## The Winchester Court of Pavilion

If the Winchester Court of Pavilion had restricted its jurisdiction to that which properly belonged to a court of piepowder there would have been no legitimate grounds for
complaint; but besides dealing with matters specifically pertaining to the fair, it took over everything that might be
thought to touch the king's peace in the city, and was indeed
the only judicial authority throughout that long term, while
the city protected its interests as best it could by having an
attorney in attendance at court, with instructions to rise and
object whenever charges were read out in cases that ought not
to be heard there. So absolute, in fact, was the assumed
authority of the Court of Pavilion, that all pleas begun before
the justices of the bishop's court and not concluded before
the end of the fair were adjourned to the vigil of St. Giles's
Day of the following year, and not, as at Hereford, passed on
to the city courts held next day.

At first, Winchester's Court of Pavilion confined its control
to the region within 7 miles of the city, which was the normal
area for a court of piepowder. Here as elsewhere, no one was
allowed to buy, sell, or offer for sale during the charter period,
merchandise of any kind, except at the fair itself. Even the
established traders and craftsmen of the city were obliged to
leave their shops and go up St. Giles's Hill to follow their
callings. Bakers might use their ovens in the city, but they
had to carry their bread to the fair before selling it. While
the fair was in progress the bishop held a special assize of
bread, wine, beer, and indeed of all victuals, which meant
that the bakers had to submit their bread for examination,
and if it was judged to be below standard they were either
fined or sentenced to the pillory by the bishop's deputy. The
inns and alehouses did remain open in the city, but the
bishop's officers might enter at any time, knock the head off
a cask without any "by your leave," and if the wine was
not to their liking demand a fine from the inn-keeper. But
extensive as an area within a radius of 7 miles was in days of
slow transport, it was not enough for the bishops of Winchester. Southampton lay outside the boundary yet near
enough for the men of that town to offer rival attractions,
particularly to the merchants who came by sea. Bishop Aymer,
therefore, while bishop-elect, entered into an agreement with

the men of Southampton by which Winchester Fair was afterwards proclaimed in Southampton also, and after this, although victuals continued to be sold as usual, everything else, on pain of forfeiture, had to be carried to Winchester and offered for sale in the streets of the fair. Southampton was thus brought within the area controlled by the bishop's court, with episcopal officers watching every road and bridge over this enlarged region, including Redbridge, Romsey, Stockbridge, Alresford and other places of entrance, in order to levy tolls and customs on all who entered Southampton as well as Winchester.

While means of distributing and selling the surplus production of a region remained inadequate within the towns themselves these annual marts were vital, and it was for this reason that the men of Southampton were willing to enter into such an apparently one-sided agreement. Nevertheless, the rapacity of the bishop and the severity of his court became increasingly intolerable to the people—buyers and sellers alike—with the result that when, at the end of the sixteen days of the fair, the mayor was allowed to reassume his authority there was always a spontaneous outburst of public rejoicing. The city minstrels, followed by a crowd of citizens, would attend the civic authorities when they went up St. Giles's Hill to reclaim the tron, which was trundled back through the bishop's soke and over St. Swithin's bridge into the city again. It was thus the end of the fair, not the beginning, that was celebrated with feasting and general rejoicing at Winchester.

The prosperity of this great fair of St. Giles continued to grow until the time of the Barons' War, when it received its first serious set-back. It is probably true to say that it never completely recovered from this. The Gascon War weakened it, reducing its turnover by one-third, and by 1350 Winchester had lost its international importance. Eleven years later much of its property, always of flimsy construction, was reported derelict, and the fair was becoming a liability rather than an asset to the bishop.

Winchester had actually received its death blow with the outbreak of the Hundred Years' War in 1337, because that had meant the end of visits by overseas buyers. And when these were no longer to be met and traded with, English merchants from such distant cities and towns as York, Beverley, Lincoln, Leicester, and Northampton lost interest. In the meantime the city itself became stronger and better able to stand up to the bishop. In 1449 the citizens were granted a fair of their own to be held for eight days from the vigil of St. Swithin. In 1518 they were granted a second fair, and the bishop's fair ultimately became redundant for commercial ends, and otherwise intolerable.

## II. St. Ives

St. Ives in Huntingdonshire is one of the smaller mediæval towns owing their entire existence to a fair, granted in this case to the abbot of Ramsey by Henry I in 1110 and confirmed by Henry III. St. Ives Easter Fair, which reached its peak in the thirteenth century, enjoyed exceptional royal patronage and may, in fact, have been procured for the abbot by the king's chamberlain, William of Houghton, who was a Huntingdonshire man and witnessed the royal signature on the first charter. The history of St. Ives, originally part of the manor of Slepe—the slippery shore, begins with the translating to Ramsey Abbey of the bones of a certain bishop of Persia named St. Ive whose story was written by one of the abbots of Ramsey during the eleventh century. A health-giving spring, or holy well, sprang from the ground close to the place of interment, and near this, Abbot Edmoth, afterwards bishop of Dorchester, founded a church, to be served by a prior and a few Benedictine monks from Ramsey. Thus it was to "St. Benedict of Ramsey and St. Ive of Slepe" that Henry I granted his fair, and as from the beginning this was for eight days, and not the customary vigil, feast, and morrow, it is clear that a very considerable unchartered fair was already flourishing as a result of the saint's renown.

So quickly did the abbot's fair grow that when, in 1252, there was a dispute about his jurisdiction it was stated that the value of the fair to the abbey exceeded that of several manors. The dispute in question was between the abbot and the king's bailiffs. The royal purchases were evidently so great at this time that in 1250 and the two following years two bailiffs were appointed to supervise them, one of whom was Roger the king's tailor, who came to the fair to buy Flemish cloth, and was in fact the biggest buyer. In 1252 these bailiffs took upon themselves to continue the fair beyond its charter length, and were themselves levying tolls, stallage, tronage, and so forth in respect of these extra days. The abbot thereupon sued them, complaining that the fair had been prolonged for three weeks longer than the charter allowed, and that as the bailiffs had continued to make all the customary fair charges during that time, they had derived far more profit than he had. To this the bailiffs replied that they disputed none of the rights and privileges enjoyed by the abbot during the eight days of the fair, but submitted that as the booths and stalls were along the king's highway, and not on a separate fair-ground as they were in most places, the king's officers had a perfect right to remain at St. Ives after the fair closed, and that all the rights of the fair must automatically revert to the king at the end of the charter period. It was the king who had appointed them, and it was on his majesty's behalf that they were receiving dues and administering justice. The abbot rejoined that although the stalls might be along the king's highway, all the property of the fair—houses, stalls, and booths—had been built by the abbey, and that no fewer than twenty monks were maintained solely for the business of the fair. Moreover, while the highway was indisputably the king's, the vessels that brought the cloth inland up the Ouse were moored on soil that was no less indisputably the abbot's.

It was from the river that the fair developed, with Bridge Street as its main thoroughfare. From this the streets shot out like branches from the parent trunk and were lined with the usual rows of stalls and booths, allocated each year to the visiting skinners, spicers, butchers, ironmongers, and the rest of them, or to towns with which one specific product or manufacture was associated, while the London merchants would be subdivided separately—the skinners with their furs, and so forth, brought to St. Ives because so much of the clothing for the royal household was bought there. "Your robes buy at St. Ives," says Bishop Grosseteste; and Miss Lilian Redstone, in her scholarly contribution on the fair, in

*Victoria County History of Huntingdonshire*, shows that in 1262 silver vessels to the value of £600 were pledged in the king's name to merchants of Douai, Ypres, and Liège for purchase at St. Ives, and that the purchases in 1237 included 1,100 ells of green and murrey cloth for knights, 180 ells of murrey for clerks, 340 ells of murrey and green for sergeants, 40 course borel gowns for grooms, 160 ells of murrey and green for ladies and damsels, as well as scarlet cloth, hoods, finer stuffs and furs. Indeed so great were the purchases year by year that in 1242 the prior of St. Ives was granted ten oaks with which to make a wardrobe for the better storage in his priory of these fine cloths bought for the royal household. A large quantity of canvas for the king's tents was bought at St. Ives in 1257 and taken to the Tower of London, and there are records of a rich variety of other commodities offered for sale there; but the principal merchandise was wool, cloth, and hides.

The dispute already mentioned concerning the abbot's rights in the fair was further complicated by the burgesses of Huntingdon also claiming the right to collect tolls, basing their claim on the rights they enjoyed throughout the county as a whole, apparently the original suit of the Huntingdon burgesses was withdrawn when a technical error in the writ was pointed out, but in 1260 they again put their rights to the test by complaining that the abbot's bailiffs prevented the Huntingdon sergeants carrying their black rods of office and collecting toll at St. Ives. These bailiffs were alleged to have confiscated the collecting boxes, and to have seized the rods and impudently snapped them before the sergeants' eyes. The quarrel appears to have continued at least until 1286, when the abbot allowed the right of the Huntingdon sergeants or bailiffs to collect toll at the gates, but not elsewhere. The game was evidently worth the candle, for at the end of the thirteenth century there were usually nine of these Huntingdon black rods in attendance, and during Edward II's reign the rolls mention four bailiffs and four sub-bailiffs.

But troublesome as these covetous burgesses were to the abbot of Ramsey, they were no worse than his rival clerics. The bishop of Ely claimed that he himself had the right to claim homage from those who traded at the fair, and

therefore should have his own bailiff in attendance, bearing a
rod of office and entitled to receive amercements and "attach-
ments." He also claimed certain dues from his own tenants
and servants who travelled to St. Ives by boat and sold beer,
oats, and fish taken from the river. This particular quarrel
increased in bitterness until in 1320 John Hotham, Bishop of
Ely, who was Edward II's chancellor, apparently got the
upper hand by obtaining from the king the grant of a fair at
Ely to last for forty days from Ascension Day, with the
privilege of requiring the sheriff of Huntingdonshire to make
a proclamation at the fair of St. Ives forbidding merchants
to remain there after Ascension Day, thus compelling them
to move their merchandise to his own fair at Ely. But by this
time the abbot of Ramsey had another card up his sleeve.
The 1252 dispute with the king's bailiffs had ended in 1258
with the granting of a new charter, by which, on payment by
the abbey of a fine of 500 marks and an annual rent of £50,
the abbot was given "the residue of the fair as long as it
should last," a most irregular grant in that it disregarded the
universally accepted rule that the duration of a fair should
be limited. However, there it was, and the king was obliged
to revoke his new grant to the bishop of Ely.

Apparently in Henry III's time the fair at St. Ives had
lasted for about four weeks; but during Edward II's it had
been extended for as long as forty days, usually ending on the
eve of Pentecost. Its organization was an elaborate business.
As at Hereford, tenants on the abbot's manors were required
to bring in bundles of rods from which the hurdles for
dividing-walls were made. It was policed by a constabulary
also provided by the abbot's manors, each of which had to
provide its constables and watchmen, while every house in
Bridge Street and the Green had to provide one watchman,
presumably to guard his own frontage.

The courts of piepowder were much concerned by the great
influx of harlots at fairtime, many of whom seem to have been
harboured by barbers. It is amusing to find that one of the
offenders in this respect was suitably named William Red-
knave. And there were all the other tricksters. At the fair in
1275 a Stamford man pleaded guilty to selling a brass ring
for $5\frac{1}{2}d.$, "saying that the said ring was of the purest gold,

40

and that he and a one-eyed man found it in the Church of St. Ives, near the Cross." [1] Goldsmiths and jewellers attended regularly and had to be carefully watched. Occasionally there would be interference from London, as when in 1291-2 the Royal Exchanger brought four men to St. Ives to guard the exits of the fair and compel every merchant as he left to empty his money bags before them so that they could make a check on counterfeit coinage.

As with Winchester, the outbreak of the Hundred Years War proved fatal. Both depended on overseas merchants. This, in fact, had long been realized, for in 1268 a far-sighted abbot had paid 120 marks to have exemption from payment of the annual rent to the king in time of war, because he foresaw that the profits would not be large enough to meet it. His concern is not surprising when we see from the records that merchants were then sailing up the Ouse with their precious merchandise from Ypres, Poperinghe, Ghent, Brabant, Malines, Amiens and St. Omer, Artois, and Douai. We meet them in the records of the abbot's court; Reginald and Arnulph, who were "Easterlings" or Hansards, Gerard of Cologne and Gottschalk of Almaine. They came to St. Ives to meet English merchants from all the cities of the kingdom, and particularly those of Lincoln, Beverley, and Leicester, who hired entire rows of booths and houses. These references to houses, incidently, are an unusual feature at St. Ives, because they were, in fact, houses, not stalls or shops. The frontages of those along Bridge Street, near the river bank, and about the Green—which, by the way, was a separate community, appointing its own watchman and with its own jury at the fair court—were the body of the fair. The houses here were let on the condition that these frontages were at the disposal of the abbot at fairtime. Naturally, use was made of the houses themselves for storage, but no buying or selling was allowed in the rear except by special licence.

When the Hundred Years War broke out the abbot's "fronts" could no longer be let, and although his bailiff continued to ride to St. Ives and proclaim the fair, it had ceased to be a mart of international fame. The houses, however, remained to form the nucleus of a town which, as a

[1] Maitland, *Select Pleas*, vol. i., p. 139.

result of its unusual origin, preserved the mediæval character
of its local government until well into the nineteenth century.
In fact no sort of municipal administration was set up at
St. Ives until it received its charter of incorporation in 1834.
Other reminders of its ancient fair survived in its families,
for aliens had settled here from time to time—most notably,
perhaps, the Brabant weavers who came in 1338 and taught
their craft to their neighbours. And so this small east-
midland town, with the statue of Oliver Cromwell in its
market place, achieved by means of its fair both character
and fame that still seem curiously unrelated to its size and
population.

### III. STURBRIDGE

Sturbridge, the greatest of all the English fairs and the
prototype of Bunyan's "Vanity Fair," was held in a field
between the Cambridge to Newmarket road and the River
Cam, about 2 miles from Cambridge market place. Sturbridge
Common, which is reached from Garlic Row, and the old
"Oyster House" are all that remain to remind us of it, apart
from the wealth of records and memories that must never be
lost. Here for centuries the Cambridge student bought and
sold his books, worked off his high spirits and squandered his
money. It was at Sturbridge in 1661 that Newton bought his
first book on astronomy, and, a few years later, the very prism
that appears in Roubillac's statue. Thorold Rogers, in his
*History of Agriculture and Prices in England*,[1] has a description of Sturbridge that might stand for all the great fairs in
their prime and could hardly be bettered: "The Venetian and
Genoese merchant," he says, "came with his precious stock
of Eastern produce, his Italian silks and velvets, his store of
delicate glass. The Flemish weaver was present with his
linens of Liège and Ghent. The Spaniard came with his stock
of iron, the Norwegian with his tar and pitch. The Gascon
vine-grower was ready to trade in the produce of his vine-
yard; and, more rarely, the richer growths of Spain, and, still
more rarely, the vintages of Greece were also supplied. The
Hanse towns sent furs and amber, and probably were the

[1] Vol. i, p. 141.

channel by which the precious stones of the East were supplied through the markets of Moscow and Novgorod." To receive this wealth of merchandise the ports of Lynn and Blakeney were open to all the vessels that bore it, while from the west, north, and south of England came the trains of pack-horses laden with tin from Cornwall, lead from Derbyshire, and iron from the forges of Sussex, along with the woolpacks that were the most precious of all.

There were other fairs at Cambridge.[1] Garlic Fair, which belonged to the prioress and nuns of St. Rhadegund, was held at the Feast of the Assumption; it continued into the nineteenth century. There was one at Rogationtide for the burgesses, and more interesting than either, the vigorously surviving Midsummer Fair still held on the common between Cambridge and Barnwell, which may well be the ancient Cambridge fair—older than Sturbridge. The name Barnwell is derived from Beornewelle, the well or spring of the champions, which means that here we may have one of the ancient fairs that sprang up spontaneously where athletic feats were performed annually at the burial place of a hero. And while thinking again of the origin of fairs, it is worth mentioning that another ancient fair in the neighbourhood, Reach Fair, at the fenward extremity of the Devil's Dyke, 7 miles from Cambridge, may well be an example of the boundary fairs mentioned in the first chapter, because here stood the River Gate between the two kingdoms.

Tradition ascribes Sturbridge's foundation to the Roman emperor Carausius, and there is a reference in *Liber Eliensis* (ii, 32) to Irish merchants bringing cloth to Cambridge, but whether to Sturbridge or Barnwell, who shall say? Their sites are within a mile or so of each other. But such early references amount to little. It is, however, possible, and indeed not improbable, that Cambridge had been known for its fair, either at Barnwell or Sturbridge, for a thousand years before the Sturbridge charter was granted by King John in 1211 to the lepers of the Hospital of St. Mary Magdalene, to be held on the vigil, feast, and morrow of the Holy Cross.

But antiquity has never been thought of as the chief point

[1] Dr. Frank Robinson, "The Ancient Fairs of Cambridge," *East Anglian Magazine*, 30th November, 1939.

of note about Sturbridge. Its prosperity is admitted to have come late, and to have owed little to the Church, the great mediæval patron of fairs. There was no shrine at Sturbridge comparable with those at Canterbury and St. Ives to draw to it hosts of suppliants and worshippers. Its principal asset was geographical. It was easily approached by sea and river from the east, while merchants from the south and west could reach it by the Icknield Way—whether the whole distance or not. And when East Anglia became the richest part of the kingdom Sturbridge provided a convenient place for the merchants of the north to meet and trade with those of Norfolk and Suffolk, while imports could be brought by river, principally from King's Lynn. No doubt the fact that it was relatively unhampered by clerical control gave it an advantage over St. Ives and Northampton, both of which it finally eclipsed. Fuller describes Sturbridge as "an amphibion, as well going on ground, as swimming by water, by the benefit of a navigable river." He has the story of a Kendal clothier travelling to London with his cloth about 1417 and having the apparent misfortune of getting it wet near Cambridge. With the idea of cutting his losses, he offered it for sale there and then, and did so well by the mishap that the following year he returned and brought others with him. "*In memoria* thereof," he says, "Kendal men challenge some privilege in that place, annually choosing one of the town to be chief, before whom an antique sword was carried, with some mirthful solemnities, disused of late, since these sad times, which put men's minds into more serious employments." If this was not, as he suggests it was, the origin of the fair, it may well have been the origin of a substantial section of it. Certainly by the middle of the fifteenth century it had drawn to itself much of the trade of Northampton, Boston, and St. Ives. The abbeys of the Midlands—of Oxfordshire and Warwickshire—as well as those of the eastern counties, were buying their victuals there.

At the Dissolution both town and university put in claims for the revenues of Sturbridge, and the value of these is made evident by the angry disputes between them until their respective rights were set out in the charter granted by Elizabeth I in 1589, which recites: "Previously to the 30th

44

Henry VIII, the mayor, bailiffs, and burgesses had from time immemorial had and used a fair called Sturbridge Fair held at Barnwell and Sturbridge, in the county of Cambridge and within the liberty of the town, beginning on the Feast of St. Bertholomew the Apostle, and continuing from thence till the fourteenth day next after the Feast of the Exaltation of the Holy Cross; which fair, from the advantages of the place, its contiguity to the University, and the fitness of the season, far surpassed the greatest and most celebrated fairs of all England; whence great benefits had resulted to the merchants of the whole kingdom, who resorted thereto, and there quickly sold their wares and merchandises to purchasers coming from all parts of the Realm." But while the town and university were frequently at loggerheads over the fair, it would be unjust to both to overlook such amicable settlements as one recorded for 1534, when "all dranke together at the Pompe Tavern and the Unyversyte payd for all."

By Elizabeth's charter the town was empowered to make regulations for the control of the fair—the setting up and taking down of its booths, its policing and general supervision —while the university was given the assize of bread, wine, ale, and beer, the supervision of weights and measures, the right of inquiry into forestalling, the right to search for and punish common women and vagabonds, and the benefit of any fines derived from the punishment of these offenders. The moral control of the fair had always been a serious problem for the university, and after this charter a night-watch was arranged by the lieutenants and commissioners of the University. Eight watchmen, wearing red coats, patrolled the fair hourly; but appear to have taken reasonable precautions against catching anybody, because in addition to their bright costume, which might have been thought warning enough, they cried out lustily "Look about you there" as they went their rounds!

The inspection of commodities was the town's responsibility, with the exceptions of leather and sackcloth, for which inspectors were appointed in equal numbers by both. Perhaps the most popular officer was a personage called Lord of the Taps, who sported a crimson coat decorated with taps, and was privileged to sample the ale. Ned Ward refers to him as going "arm'd all over with spiggots and fossets, like a porcupine with his quills, or looking rather like a fowl wrapped up in a pound of sausages." But the high-light of the fair was the proclamation on St. Bartholomew's Day, when a procession came out of Cambridge headed by the Town Crier in scarlet, mounted, followed by twenty-eight petty constables on foot. Drums, banners, and streamers preceded the principal figure, the Grand Marshal, while behind him walked two trumpeters, the Town Music, two French horns, and the bellman. Then came the Town Clerk, mounted, with the mayor or the vice-chancellor next—according to which was to have the privilege of opening the fair—mounted on a richly caparisoned horse led by two footmen called red-coats, who carried in their free hand the familiar wands of office. Finally, in the rear of the procession, came the twenty-four Common Councillors riding three and three abreast according to seniority, the eight Dispensers in their gowns, and the gentlemen and tradesmen of the town.

This splendid civic occasion always ended in a banquet, at which fresh herrings were the principal dish. Other fare traditionally associated with Sturbridge was roast goose, which came into season at the fair—appropriately, since it ended at noon on Michaelmas Day—and roast and boiled pork, while on horse-fair day, the 14th September, Colchester oysters and fresh herrings were always on the menu. The Cambridge records have many items to remind us of Sturbridge festivities. From 1630, for example, we have:

> Item, for muzitions at the maiors booth at Sturbridge faier, iiij s.
> Item, to hym that shewed the dancinge horse before the Maior & Aldermen, v s.
> Item, paid old Hall for whippinge of Rogues, xx d.

The dancing horse referred to was probably that most celebrated of performing steeds, Bankes's horse, Morocco, which figures in Shakespeare, Ben Jonson, Sir Walter Raleigh, John Donne, Bishop Hall, Taylor the Water Poet, and a host of lesser writers.

Horse-fair day was always the most popular, and had its own mock ceremonial called christening, or initiating, which was performed at the "Robin Hood" inn. The candidate, or freshman, was introduced to the senior members in the inn parlour. Sponsors were chosen, and the candidate was then placed in an armchair ready for the ceremony to commence. The officiating dignitary, robed in Cambridge cap and gown, entered the room with a bell in one hand and a book in the other, attended by two vergers holding staves and lighted candles. But the principal attraction of the ceremony was the Christening cup, which was, of course, a bowl of punch!

It was one of the proctors' duties at the fair "to seek out and punish lewd women," who, as we should imagine, were never far to seek. When caught, they were imprisoned in the Spinning House. "Thither," says Carter the Cambridge historian, "doth the Toun Cryer oft-tymes resort, to discipline the Ladies of Pleasure with his whip." No doubt the parson of Barnwell had these ladies well in mind when he visited the fair to call the people to repentance from what Ned Ward describes as an "old weather-beaten pulpit, where on Sunday a sermon is delivered for the edification of the strolling sinners, who give open attention, as in a field conventicle." These Sturbridge sermons were one of the features of the fair, and no doubt the parson was often as good a showman as any of the motley crew that composed his strange congregation.

The classic description of Sturbridge is Defoe's, although in reading him we ought always to bear in mind William Minto's warning: "De Foe was a great, truly great, liar; perhaps the greatest liar that ever lived." [1] Defoe tells us that it was kept in a large cornfield extending from the River Cam towards the road, with the rivulet from which it takes its name on the east, and that it covered about half a mile square. Each year, he says, there was a scramble among the farmers to get in their corn before the proclamation on the 24th August, otherwise it was trampled down and lost. But they had generous compensation at the end in the manure left behind by the thousands of horses. The fair people at the other end of the period had to be as quick off the mark as the farmers had been at the beginning, because on the 14th September the ploughs went in whether the field was clear or not.

[1] Minto: *Defoe, English Man of Letters.*

# The Four Great Fairs of England

The setting up of such a fair as Sturbridge must have been an amazing spectacle. All the facilities of a large and prosperous shopping town were provided overnight with every imaginable trade represented—"in a word," says Defoe, "all trades that can be named in London; with coffee-houses, taverns, brandy-shops, and eating-houses, innumerable, and all in tents and booths," The main street of the fair ran for nearly half a mile from the road northward to the bank of the Cam at Chesterton. In the centre was the great square called the Duddery, so named from the commodities sold there, where the booths or tents were exceptionally large and spaced to allow great wagons to come in and both load and unload. They were more like enormous warehouses, and were, in fact, designed for the wholesale business of the fair. Here, Defoe tells us, a hundred thousand pounds worth of merchandise would be sold in the course of a week, apart from the business done by the agents and merchants who transacted their business "wholly in their pocket-books," and whose sales were said to exceed that in which goods changed hands on the actual ground.

When we think of the hazards of transport before modern roads were made, we can hardly imagine how it was possible for these enormous quantities of woven cloth from Halifax, Leeds, Wakefield, Huddersfield and the villages of the mountainous Pennine country in both Lancashire and Yorkshire to be transported safely to the fens of East Anglia. Trains of packhorses were used, and all these had to be stalled and fed. One warehouse alone visited by Defoe had twenty thousand pounds worth of goods in it—at 1720 prices! And not only were cloths brought in from the north. From the West Country came kerseys, druggets, shalloons, cantaloons, and the rest of the products of the villages about Exeter, Taunton, and Bristol. But to Defoe's way of thinking the two staple commodities were wool and hops, which took their price for the season from what they fetched at Sturbridge Fair. These came from both Chelmsford in Essex and Farnham in Surrey, but principally from Canterbury and Maidstone. These, as well as all London goods, came by water, first to King's Lynn, and from there by barge up the Ouse and Cam to the field itself. But in addition there was iron and brass to be brought

48

from Birmingham, knives and edged tools from Sheffield, glassware from Nottingham and hosiery from Leicester. As for the customers, fifty hackney coaches plied night and morning between London and Cambridge, and, to Defoe's astonished delight, wherries—the eighteenth-century equivalent of our modern water-buses—were brought from London on wagons to plie upon the Cam between Cambridge and Sturbridge.

To accommodate this great concourse of people all the surrounding towns and villages took in their quota of lodgers. Barns and stables were turned into inns, while the stallholders had to eat, drink and sleep in their booths or tents for reasons of security as well as for lack of other accommodation. Eating booths were everywhere, and each morning butchers and higglers would come in from the neighbouring counties as well as towns with plentiful supplies for all. "In a word," says Defoe, "the fair is like a well fortify'd city, and there is the least disorder and confusion (I believe) that can be seen anywhere, with so great a concourse of people."

As was the custom at most fairs, the wholesale business was done first. Then came the day for the gentry, and it was to them that the retailers looked most hopefully. The horse-fair came at the end, when there was time for sports and races for the enlivenment of "the meaner sort."

The enthusiasm of the genial eighteenth-century squire, Jacob Butler, who used to entertain its giants and dwarfs, kept the fair going in the later part of the eighteenth century, but it gradually declined, and the vice-chancellor "called the fair" at Sturbridge for the last time on the 18th September, 1855, although it continued to be proclaimed by the mayor until 1933. The Cambridge *Daily News* for the 25th September, 1930, reported that his worship, accompanied by the four bailiffs, the town crier, the sergeant-at-arms, and the town clerk, had proclaimed the fair the previous day in the presence of not more than half a dozen onlookers, who were rewarded with bright new halfpennies. The fair that year consisted of no more than a single traction engine with a cargo of swing boats. The following year even these were missing, and the audience was made up of only two police officers and three men. Whether or not these were given new halfpennies for

49

their pains is not reported. The final opening is happily recorded by Mrs. Keynes in her *Byways of Cambridge History*. She herself was mayor of Cambridge in 1933, and, attended by the Clerk of the Peace and the sergeant-at-arms, she performed the proclamation ceremony for the last time. There was one ice-cream barrow on the ground, and the audience was composed of two women with babies in arms. Thus ended the great fair which at one time was both the busiest mart in the realm and the merriest rout.

### IV. BARTHOLOMEW FAIR

> There double beere and bottle-ale
> In everie corner had good sale:
> Many a pig, and many a sow,
> Many a jade, and many a cow:
> Candle rushes, cloth and leather,
> And many things came in together:
> Many a pound and penny told,
> Many a bargaine bought and sold.

Such was "Old Bartlemy" with its swarms of stout beggars, its pimps, bawds, and cutpurses, as Ben Jonson celebrated its fame, when Adam Overdo, justice of its court of piepowder, walked its streets in the habit of a fool so that he could hear and see for himself the enormities that cried for correction.

It had been yet another of Henry I's grants of fairs to the greater churches of England, and this time the merry antics were not inappropriate. The priory of St. Bartholomew the Great was founded by that "pleasant witted gentleman," Rahere, the king's jester, of whom it has been engagingly recorded that he "ofte hawnted the Kyng's palice, and amo'ge the noyseful presse of that tumultous courte, enforsed himself with jolite and carnal suavitie: ther yn spectaclis, yn metys, yn playes, and other courtely mokkys and trifyllis intrudying, he lede forth the besynesse of alle the day." This artful, if pious, founder introduced the usual relics and tales—fables it is to be feared—of miracles, and thus ensured for his foundation a constant flow of grateful or suppliant pilgrims.

Rahere's is an old story. Weary of the vanities of court, he

50

prayed that a worthier life might be offered him, and in
answer the Apostle Bartholomew came to him in a vision
and bade him build a priory at Smithfield, where he might
live, with such monks as would join him, the life of prayer
and charity. Rahere obeyed the apostle and was himself made
prior; but the jester was not dead in him. The clown must
have his public, and in order to attract attention to his priory
Rahere put out tales of cures and miracles performed at the
altar in his church, and though he was eventually denounced
as an impostor the public were not be to undeceived. The
jester's fair, chartered in 1133, ten years after the foundation
of the priory, outlived the saint's and the merchant's, and
was only suppressed after prolonged agitation in 1855, by
which time it had flourished for more than seven hundred
years.

Every component of a fair was there from the beginning,
every manifestation and expression of its piety, its feasting,
its greed, its folly—and all, it seems, in melodramatic proportions. We have the rabble of sick and diseased gabbling
their prayers at the altar, the chapmen haggling in the porch,
pedlars crying their wares and chaffering in the churchyard,
minstrels, mummers, and acrobats—or tumblers—with clerks
and friars going among them to beg alms, and the way being
cleared every few seconds for a mounted knight or dignitary
of the Church to ride through, all to the accompaniment of
the lowing of oxen, the neighing of horses, and the bleating
of sheep. Slaves were bought and sold here as well as the
cloth on which the wealth of the priory was ultimately to
depend. Nearby, at Skinners' Well, the Company of Parish
Clerks performed their miracle plays, sometimes before the
king and his court and usually with nobility present. And it
is more than likely that the first plays at St. Bartholomew's
Fair, for which long afterwards the London theatres were to
close, were representations of the miracles that Rahere the
jester alleged had been performed in his church? These would
be succeeded by "mysteries," which in turn were followed
by "moralities," while just outside the priory gates, on the
site of the fair—or part of the site—were the martyr fires, the
most lurid and terrible spectacle of all. Henry Morley, the
historian of the fair, reminds us of one of the most frightful

of these spectacles, that in 1305, when on the first day of the fair the people surged across the green to the gallows under the elms, and there saw Sir William Wallace, the hero of Scottish independence, who had been brought to London in chains the previous day and had been tried and condemned that morning, dragged into Smithfield at the tails of horses, hanged for a while and, before the breath had gone out of his body, cut down and disembowelled before being burned. Bartholomew's is not a pretty story. These burnings were to continue till 1611.

At the Dissolution, Rahere's priory fell into the hands of a man no less cunning, Sir Richard Rich, who as Chancellor of the Court of Augmentations, knew which of the plums were worth slipping into his own bag. Rich was the son and grandson of London mercers. He "bought" the priory, with all its rights, and established himself in the prior's house. In order that there should be no doubt about his title to the revenues of the fair, now called "Cloth Fair," a new charter was drawn up in his favour, and he and his heirs had a fortune by it. Two years after the granting of this charter we get our first eye-witness account of Bartholomew's Fair in the *Itinerarium* of Paul Hentzer, a German tutor who visited England in 1598, and whose account was printed by Horace Walpole at Strawberry Hill in 1757. It had already lost its importance as a cloth fair, but Hentzer describes the ceremonial of the lord mayor's proclamation and the fun and games that followed. Its traditional association with their craft was then and long afterwards celebrated by the city tailors, who, the evening before the official opening, assembled at the "Hand and Shears" in Cloth Fair, which remains to this day an authentic bit of mediæval London, and from there marched, shears in hand, to the Priory Gate, where they went through a mock ceremonial of their own, concluding with what was called "the snapping of the shears." The court of piepowder had long been held at the "Hand and Shears," and this mock ceremonial of the city tailors was to commemorate the annual visit to Bartholomew Cloth Fair of the Merchant Tailors, who brought with them the silver yard-stick by which all measures used at the stalls were checked.

There was little of Cloth Fair left for Ben Jonson to

describe in his hilarious *Bartholomew Fair*. Apparently "Bartlemy" was mainly an affair of guzzling in his day. There was always an ox roasted whole—as there should be at every big fair, piping-hot slices of which were sold to greedy spectators who were probably overfed and overheated already. The smell of roast-pig was everywhere. And no doubt there was ale enough to wash it down. "Bartlemy" was no place for delicate nostrils. No wonder Evelyn was shocked by it. And no wonder Pepys enjoyed it mightily—"Went twice round Bartholomew Fair," he wrote on the 28th August, 1667, "which I was glad to see again." Two days later he repeated the visit. "I went to Bartholomew Fair," he says of this occasion, "to walk up and down: and there, among other things, find my Lady Castlemaine at a puppet-play (*Patient Grisel*), and a street full of people expecting her coming out." Lady Castlemaine had a personal interest in the fair, because when not with the king, she was as likely as not to be found with Jacob Hall, the rope-dancer, who was one of the fair's prime favourites. One of his handbills will give an idea of the kind of thing offered by the fair at this date:

"These are to give Notice to all Gentlemen and Others, That there is joyned together Two of the Best Companies in England, *viz.* Mr. Jacob Hall (Sworn Servant to his Majestie), and Mr. Richard Lancaster, with several Others of the Companies; by Whom will be performed Excellent Dancing and Vaulting on the Ropes; with Variety of Rare Feats of Activity and Agility of Body upon the Stage; as doing of Somersets, and Flip-flaps, Flying over Thirty Rapiers, and over several Men's heads; and also flying through severall Hoops: Together with severall other Rare Feats of Activity, that will be there presented: with the Witty Conceits of Merry Will: in the performing of all which They Challenge all Others whatsoever, whether Englishmen or Strangers, to do the like with them for Twenty Pounds, or what more They please."

Large red noses were the favourite objects of ridicule just then, probably with Oliver Cromwell's inflated member in mind. Morality plays were still performed, along with such representations of classical scenes as *The Siege of Troy*, or *The Loves of Hero and Leander*, the one Ben Jonson chooses for the last act of his play. Performing animals were also

popular. One of Ben's characters says: "I have been at the
Eagle and the Black Wolf, and the Bull with the five legs,
and the Dogs that dance the Morrice, and the Hare with the
Tabor." The scenes at Bartholomew Fair had long been
vulgar; but with the Restoration they became gross in the
extreme. The closing of the theatres during the Commonwealth had reduced drama to groundling level, and when
Charles II extended the fair from three to fourteen days
every broken-down old actor in the country decked himself
out in any rag of a costume he could find and made his way
to Smithfield. Its licentiousness was to go unchecked until
1708, when the Court of Common Council again reduced its
duration to the traditional three days. But enormous booths
continued to go up each year from about 1714, when theatrical
performances became extremely popular, and as late as 1769
it was still necessary to have seventy-two officers specially
appointed to keep that precious peace which had always been
boasted of as incident to every fair by right of its charter.

Fielding the novelist, was long believed to have been a
Bartholomew showman with a booth in George Yard. He and
Reynolds, the actor, were said to have had several successful
seasons there, and to have produced the *Beggar's Opera* with
a company drawn from the Haymarket. An advertisement in
the *Daily Post* of the 23rd August, 1729, informs the public
that:

"At Mr. Fielding's Great Theatrical Booth in the George
Inn Yard in Smithfield, during the time of Bartholomew Fair,
will be acted a diverting Dramatic Opera called 'Hunter, or
the Beggar's Wedding,' with Alterations, consisting of a
variety of English, Scots, and Irish Ballad Tunes, with addi-
tional Songs never perform'd therein before. N.B. the Booth
is very commodious, and the Inn Yard has all the con-
veniences of Coach room, Lights, &c., for Quality and others,
and shall perform this evening, at Four, and every day during
the time of the Fair; beginning exactly at Two o'clock, and
continuing every hour till Eleven at Night." The Mr. Fielding
concerned, however, as Austin Dobson pointed out, was not,
as had formerly been assumed, Henry the novelist, but a
Timothy Fielding.

The appeal in the eighteenth century was still to the

"quality," and it is evident that the fair continued to enjoy the patronage even of the nobility. The last royal visit recorded is that of the Duke and Duchess of Gloucester in 1778. Sir Robert Walpole, wearing the Star, appears in Satchel's print, and it seems clear that in the eighteenth century there was a return, if only temporary, to something at least resembling respectability, which, no doubt, was due to the improved status enjoyed by the theatre at this time. Fielding's was not the only booth for the "quality," and many actors and actresses who were afterwards the darlings of theatre audiences first made their names at Bartholomew Fair. Penkethman the elder boasted the title, "The Flower of Bartholomew Fair." Quin, Cibber, Macklin, and Edward Shuter followed. On 30th August, 1732, the *Daily Post* reported that, "Yesterday the Prince and Princess went to Bartholomew Fair, and saw Mr. Fielding's celebrated droll called the 'Earl of Sussex' and the 'Forced Physician' and were so well pleased as to stay and see it twice performed." But the fair is chiefly associated with such of the old comic actors as Tom Dogget, who "wore a farce in his face," and did a star turn called "The Cheshire Round." William Bullock of York is censured by Steele for "gagging." His was the largest booth in 1739. Then there was Cadman, whose terrifying flights on the rope were immortalized by Hogarth, while the favourite Merry Andrew was William Phillips.

In the eighteenth century also there was a revival of the old mystery plays, and of those representations of such Biblical scenes as the Creation and Noah's Flood, for which the fair had been known in the Middle Ages, particularly of those in which animals could be introduced. It was, in fact, from this revival of stories of the Creation that circuses came into vogue. And at the same time the introduction of machinery made possible more dramatic presentations of such scenes as Dives rising out of Hell and Lazarus in Abraham's bosom, which became popular again.

The final breakdown came in 1839, when the City of London doubled the charges for space—raising Wombwell's rent, for example, from £40 to £80 a year—and thus crippled the showmen. In the same year the London City Missions Society presented a petition for its suppression, and the City Lands

Committee was instructed to consider whether this could legally be accomplished. The question, of course, was referred to the city solicitor, who was asked to report to the Markets Committee "as to the right of the Corporation of London to suppress Bartholomew Fair, or otherwise to remove the nuisances and obstructions to trade to which it gives rise." He gave a carefully guarded answer expressing the opinion, that as the right to hold fairs had been granted for the purpose of promoting trade, there could be no prescriptive right for committing any nuisance that was incompatible with the purpose for which it had been granted, and that the Corporation was entitled to protect the public by confining the fair to its original object and purpose, and so forth. The Lord Mayor, however, continued to read the proclamation until 1850, but after 1840 with only the minimum of ceremonial consistent with the dignity of his office. Subsequently it was read by a deputy until the fair was abolished in 1855. Few, apparently, regretted its disappearance. A letter in *The Times* of 5th September, 1796, gives what was even then the general view of the educated Londoner:

"The various troupes of itinerant comedians, showmen, rope-dancers, jugglers, conjurers, fortune-tellers, giants, dwarfs, wild beasts, learned beasts, and every *lusus naturæ* that can be collected throughout the kingdom, with all the appendages of immorality and vice, were on Saturday put in legal possession of Smithfield, as the theatre of their achievements. When we add to these the numerous tribe of pick-pockets, ring droppers, and sharpers of every description, we cannot but . . . lament that the Chief Magistrate of the City of London should be annually compelled to degrade his dignity as the principal guardian of the public peace and morals, by going in state to license a scene which terminates in the most fatal abuses."

What it amounts to is that London had outgrown "Old Bartlemy" and lost the stomach for its full-blooded coarseness and horse-play.

## CHAPTER IV

# Fairs into Markets

THE primary difference between fairs and markets, that
the one have a yearly, the other a weekly, regulation,
implies more than a mere calendar distinction. It implies
that unlike markets, fairs were originally for the exchange of
commodities on the grand scale and flourished in a society in
which the people were largely self-supporting in their day-
to-day needs—a society in which the buyers and sellers were
not small householders, as they became for the most part at
markets, but princes, nobles, and the heads of monastic
houses. Long after the needs of townspeople in general were
being met by regular markets, such families as the Howards,
Nevilles, Percies, and Stanleys continued to restock their
castles and manors at the annual fairs, some of which they
owned, while the monasteries continued to lay in their stocks
at Sturbridge, Winchester, and St. Ives till the Dissolution,
even though most of them must long before then have had
market towns within easy reach. And there is a similar distinction in their siting, because place as well as time is a
primary factor with markets no less than with fairs. While

fairs were either outside towns, or superimposed on them to the suspension of their normal life, markets were contained by the towns and regulated by their needs. Both, however, had their rise in feudal and ecclesiastical times, and began under despotic control, which the great fairs, as international marts, did not survive, while the markets did.

Although it is true that markets were largely to displace fairs for the internal commerce of the country, this does not necessarily mean that the one had a longer or more important history than the other. They had existed together since Saxon times, markets for small-scale, fairs for large-scale, trading, and both had to be carefully regulated from the beginning on the principle of the Roman maxim, *ubi est multitudo, ibi esse rector*—where there is a crowd someone should be responsible for its control. So from as early as the ninth century we find laws for the peaceful and orderly conduct of markets being made, which ordained that all transactions involving more than a certain sum should be in the presence of trustworthy witnesses, who would be able to give evidence in case of dispute. In the early days of barter, of course, time and place for the witnessing of transactions would not be decreed, but as trading increased it became convenient, and ultimately essential, for it to be done at agreed times and places. Thus the necessity for markets arose, and the simplest way of controlling them in the circumstances of mediæval life was to grant them, as fairs were granted, to the lord of the manor in which they were held. Again as with fairs, although there had been laws regulating them since Saxon times, their strict control came with the Conqueror, who enacted that no market or fair should be held except in cities and walled towns, or where there were castles or other secure places "where the customs of our kingdom and our common law and the dignities of our Crown, which have been constituted by our good predecessors, cannot perish, or be defrauded or violated," so that all things should "be done regularly and openly and by judgment and justice."

At the outset, the modest revenue the lord of the manor would derive from these gatherings would be no more than a modest—perhaps hardly an adequate—return for the services he provided. In later centuries, however, when large towns developed round an ancient cross or market square as the result of these markets, the sole rights of which were vested in the owner of the franchise, profit and expenditure lost all relationship with each other, and the private ownership of the public market became a genuine cause of grievance.

The rigid enforcement of the Norman law had been relaxed by the thirteenth century and men had come to buy and sell freely in places that did not fulfil the Conqueror's conditions. But already a market franchise had become a valuable possession, and the granting of new ones was jealously watched. Before a new market was granted a jury was sworn to decide whether it was likely to hurt either the king or a neighbouring owner. Thus in 1261 we find Richard Earl of Cornwall bringing an action against Maurice Lord Berkeley for damaging with his market and fair at Wenden in Essex the earl's market and fair at Newport, and a similar complaint—to be matched where you will—in 1222 about the detrimental effect of the new market at Watchet on the one at Dunster.

The first question to be asked was whether the place for which the new market was sought was $6\frac{2}{3}$ miles away from the next, that being the operative radius of a franchise. This apparently odd distance was based on the assumption that 20 miles was a full day's walk. By dividing this into three parts, equal amounts of time and energy were allowed for those who lived farthest away, which meant that those who lived near had a considerable advantage. For all that, trade and travel in the Middle Ages were much more likely to be governed by the duration of daylight than by arbitrary divisions of time and distance.

With Edward III came a change of policy. No longer were security and the guarding of ancient rights of prime importance. These gave way to the demands of the expanding wool trade so vigorously promoted by the king, which in course of time was to raise up the new class of wealthy merchants who eventually displaced the feudal nobles in many parts of the country. Working through gilds, the wool magnates developed the markets granted in great number by Edward as a means of liberating trade from the autocratic and mercenary owners of the greater fairs, both lay and clerical, until eventually the gilds—such is our common nature—themselves became as despotic and avaricious as the nobles and clerics they supplanted. But that is another story. Meanwhile the attitude to trade itself changed. Protection against fraud was still important, but less vital than the necessity of providing frequent and regular assemblies of buyers and sellers, whose keenness would ensure that commodities found their natural price. Trading, in short, was becoming part and parcel of the nation's everyday life instead of an annual or biannual renewal and adjustment of it. Inevitably there was a loss of colour and excitement in this, although the "dark stranger" was always to be found somewhere in the market—that is to say, alongside the local goodman and his wife, who stood at the market cross behind their baskets of butter and eggs, there would be a wandering chapman or two to give mystery and romance to the scene. Such have always been found in our markets, from the "dark Phœnicians" who carried their packs along the prehistoric trackways of England to those dusky visitors of to-day who keep up a kind of incantation behind their wares, running through variations of: "You have a lucky face, sir. Maybe I bring you luck. Here is a tie just your colour, sir. Yes, lady. You have a lucky . . ." and so on interminably.

The most popular day for markets in the Middle Ages was Sunday. As fairs were linked with the annual festivals of the Church it is not surprising that the ordinary weekly assemblies for worship should have been accepted as the most suitable time for markets, nor that the churchyard, and sometimes the church building, should have been thought the most suitable place. Nevertheless, there appear to have been stirrings of conscience about the practice in Saxon times, and in 1172 what was probably the earliest determined attempt to introduce a different day was made. It was inspired by an incident recorded by Giraldus Cambrensis, who tells us that as Henry II passed through Cardiff on his way from Ireland that year he heard mass in St. Perian's Chapel, and as he was leaving an old man came up to him and cried: "God help thee, O King! Christ and His Holy Mother, John the Baptist and Peter the Apostle greet thee, and by me order thee to forbid all fairs and markets on the Lord's Day, and all unnecessary labours . . . so shalt thou prosper." When asked by whose authority he spoke, the man repeated the words, warning the king that unless he paid heed to the message, "before a year shall pass away harder things shall happen to thee, which so long as thou livest thou shalt not shake off." The strongest movement against Sunday trading, however, came as a result of the preaching of Eustace, Abbot of Flaye, who came to England on a special mission from the Pope with the specific object of bringing sanctity to the first day. Evidently the Continent was ahead of England in Sunday observance at this time. At first the movement appears to have been successful. Peterborough, Oundle, and Rothwell were among the many towns that switched their markets from Sunday to Saturday. But the reform was short-lived, and in Henry III's reign another attempt had to be made, which resulted in a considerable group of towns adopting Saturday as market day. Among them were Berkhamstead, Wallingford, Wimborne, Leominster, Clare, Warkworth, with many others, and undoubtedly the movement would have been far more successful than it was if the market-owning clergy had not been so reluctant to support it. The bishop of Salisbury had Sunday markets at Warminster and Ramsbury, the abbot a Sunday market at Abbotsbury, and Battle kept its Sunday market till the Dissolution. That Sunday was much the most profitable day is proved repeatedly, particularly in such presentments for forestalling as that of the wife of Henry Lant, who bought poultry in the Saturday market at Norwich and sold it the following day at the gate of Holy Trinity church, "whereof great outcry has arisen." [1]

As for the other offence, that of holding markets in or about churches, we again find eminent clerics among the most persistent offenders. Booths were set up regularly in Ely Cathedral for the sale of St. Audrey's laces. In 1150 the bishop of Wells complained about the holding of fairs and markets in the precincts of the cathedral,[2] yet they continued to be held in parish churches, if not also in cathedrals, until in the thirteenth century we find Robert Grosseteste, Bishop of Lincoln, showing that he meant business by not only

---

[1] W. Hudson, Ed., *Leet Jurisdiction in the City of Norwich* (13th cent.), Seldon Society, vol. v (1891).
[2] Somerset Arch. Soc. lv. 92.

complaining about them but expressly forbidding them. But the offence, of course, was much less shocking to the mediæval mind than it is to the modern. There was little reverence for the church building before Laud's time, and apart from that, when travelling was extremely hazardous and opportunities for trading were few there might even have been hardship in remote parts of the country if these Sunday markets had been abolished forthwith. Moreover, everyone knew how hard it is to amend the settled habits of the people. Sunday trading, it would be argued, would go on whether legally or illegally, and if illegally then tolls would be lost, as they were at Cockermouth in Cumberland, where, in 1306, it was complained that every Sunday there was a gathering (*congregatio*) of people buying and selling wares and thus evading the dues at Cockermouth market. There was no question about Sunday being the most popular day. Nor was there any question about the Church and its immediate vicinity being the most popular place. So when the hucksters had been driven out of the nave they clung to the porch and churchyard, where markets continued to be held in some outlying places until the eighteenth century. The very large porches we find in many small churches were built with secular assemblies in mind.

Gradually, however, the market folk moved outward, first setting their stalls in a circle round what had now come to be regarded as the sacred enclosure, the churchyard, and later along the broad way leading to the church, where the shops that succeeded them were eventually to form the centre of the town—the market place, or high street, with the Church at the head, and perhaps a market cross in the centre. In this way markets determined the physical form of the new trading communities that succeeded the manors, although for a long time marketing did in fact remain severely manorial, and there are survivals of it even to-day. The effect of the change —which of course came gradually—was to establish a new regional basis for the distribution of commodities, which eventually made it possible for the region to supersede the manor as the basis of local government. In the purely agricultural community the process was simple. At Eye in Suffolk, for example, the town was evolved from the manor as the inhabitants by trading gained capital, and finally were able to commute feudal conditions of tenure for a money rent. In such towns it was the market, and the market alone, that enabled a village community to bridge the gap between manorial servitude and borough freedom, particularly where a local industry could be introduced, and in course of time organized into a gild. This kind of development is seen best in the wool towns of East Anglia and the Cotswolds.

In later times it was more often the town that produced the market than the market that produced the town, particularly at the time of the Industrial Revolution. Communities of people engaged in industry and no longer self-supporting required a regular supply of food, which had to be brought in from the country, and this regular supply of fresh food has, of course, been the heart and soul of marketing ever since. And what colour and vitality our towns have derived from this weekly mingling of country folk and townsfolk! George Eland illustrates this neatly in the introduction to his *Purefoy Letters*,[1] where he tells us how Henry Purefoy, an eighteenth-century gentlemen would note that he met in Brackley on market day not only his country friends but "Mr. Yates, the shopkeeper; the old beggar woman; Master Fenimore, senior, the glazier; Mr. Cooper, the schoolmaster; the man who sells hats next to Mr. Yates's; Mr. Strank's man and boy; the Landlady and man and servants at the Red Lion Inn; Will Loveday, 'wee bought the pigs on'; the Biddlesden man who drove the pigs home; Mrs. Blencow, the orange woman, and many others."

It is interesting to note that although rising industrial towns sought and obtained market charters from Tudor times, they received them quite independently of their rights as municipalities. In England they were never, as they were in Scotland, an integral part of a trading town. In most towns markets were already established, and eventually had to be bought at great cost to the community from the holder of the charter, although in most cases he and his forebears had done very little to develop either the market or the town. It was the apparent injustice of many of these old market rights in the circumstances created by the Industrial Revolution, that led Charles Bradlaugh, on the 22nd April, 1887, to move

[1] Sidgwick and Jackson, 1931.

in the House of Commons that a Royal Commission be set up to inquire how many markets were still in private hands, how they were managed, and to report on the advisability of compulsorily transferring them to local authorities. In the course of his speech he said that Manchester had paid £200,000 in 1846 for market rights and property, of which it was estimated that as much as £170,000 was for the manorial rights alone, yet so inadequate was the market that having acquired it at this enormous cost Manchester had to spend a further £359,000 on modernizing the facilities. In Bradford the market rights were acquired on lease for a rent of £5,000 a year, although there the market was held in the open streets. Bradlaugh argued that as this £5,000 a year had to be taken from the ratepayers it was, in effect, a tax on the people for the benefit of the market-holders, who had done nothing whatever to create this valuable asset. The asset had, in fact, been created by the people who were having to buy it. So ambiguous were some of these alleged rights that apparently no one was able to define them. A private market owner at Ware in Hertfordshire was found to be illegally levying tolls on all cattle coming over the bridge to his market.

As the result of Bradlaugh's motion the Royal Commission was granted by the Government, and its Report, completed in 1891, is the most valuable document we have on fairs and markets. Unfortunately it is not in a form that can be quickly digested or summarized.

But it was not only a question of who was entitled to the profits. The paramount importance of the market was that it supplied the people's food, and as the industrial population grew, the regulation of that supply increased in complexity, while the ever rising standards of living required stricter and stricter supervision of quality and measure. As early as the tenth century Edgar had decreed that all standards of weight and measure should correspond with those of Winchester and London. Magna Carta had stipulated that there should be "One measure of wine throughout the realm and one measure of corn," as well as one breadth of cloth and a uniform system of weights, yet it was only when towns came under the authority of a mayor and corporation that anything approaching uniformity was achieved. Even then there were frequent trials of strength. As late as 1569 the Manchester $\frac{1}{4}$ hundred-weight was still 30 pounds instead of 28, and a gill is $\frac{1}{2}$ not $\frac{1}{4}$ pint in parts of Lancashire to this day.

On assuming office the mayor took over the official beam and steelyard, a yard-measure, and a bushel, and swore that he would "keep truly correction on all bakers and brewers and taverners and cooks and suchlike people," and on all who used such illegal measures as "horn or aim of hand." Even the wealthy merchants of the Staple were required to bring their merchandise to be weighed at the town Balance and pay their fee to the "Fermour of the Beme." The humbler folk—bakers and brewers—were fined for the first offences; but if these were "grievous and often" the baker was sentenced to the pillory, the brewer to the tumbrel, both of which instruments of correction were kept ready in the market place.

Of the various purveyors of essential foods the bakers, it was found, were most amenable to control. The reason for this was that most of the people could bake their own bread and were therefore independent. Butchers on the other hand were in so strong a position that they could even afford to have grievances of their own, the commonest of which was against their country competitors being allowed to sell in the town market.

Originally the office of Clerk of the Market, by this time held by the mayor of every chartered borough, had been in one person only, the Clerk of the Market of the King's Household, an ancient officer of the Crown whose duty it was to regulate the permanent market kept for the supply of the royal household—a method of provisioning which was abandoned in the time of Edward I. Later he was charged with responsibility for weights and measures wherever the king might be, and to perform his duties travelled with the Court and exercised authority at all markets within the Verge, which was a region extending 12 miles outward from where the Court happened to be. By the middle of the seventeenth century, however, his jurisdiction had been extended over the entire country, and the duties were farmed out in each county on terms which inevitably led to extortion, an evil that was corrected in 1640 by an Act again restricting the Clerk's jurisdiction to the Verge, and entrusting the office elsewhere to the mayor or chief officer of the city or borough where the market was held, and in other places to the lord of the franchise or his deputy.

It was a most unpopular office. And not surprisingly! When his authority covered the realm, the Clerk of the Market could ride into any town he pleased with a troop of horsemen carrying weights and measures stamped with the sign of the Exchequer, require all the town's weights and measures to be brought to him, and when his inquiry was completed order a fresh relay of horses—not more than six —to carry him to the next town of his choice.

It cannot be denied that supervision of markets was a tricky business—as indeed it still is. A quarrel between the Church and the local authority in Canterbury lasted throughout the whole of the fifteenth century. The monks, it was alleged, tried to evade tolls by more or less smuggling their fish into the priory without its passing through the market at all. This was finally overcome in 1500 by the removal of the market from its old site near the prior's gate to one near the city church, so that there would be a space between market and priory, and the mayor would be able to keep a check on what the monks carried away. Some of the records of old market tricks make entertaining reading—soft woollen cloth being lengthened by hard rolling, an offence mentioned in *Piers Plowman*; calf skin being sold for ox leather; candles being sold without wicks; and so forth. When discovered, the pedlar would throw the blame for his misdemeanour on a servant, who, as a poor man, got off lightly. To remedy this, masters were made responsible for their servants' misdeeds, which resulted in a new injustice. To-day we have a reminder of this in companies being fined for offences committed by employees entirely on their own initiative.

Other regulations were for the control of the "regrator" and the "forestaller," ancestors of the wholesalers, or middlemen, who have always been viewed with suspicion, but whose function became necessary in most trades when large populations had to be assured of a regular flow of commodities at prices not subject to the sudden fluctuations inevitable in a market entirely dependent on the local producer. The first of several acts for the punishment of those who bought goods on the way to market was passed in the reign of Edward III, and not until July, 1844, was the last of them repealed.

As markets increased in size the mayor was no longer able to attend to everything, and overseers, or market-lookers as they were usually called, were elected to assist him. By the middle of the sixteenth century Manchester, for example, had four lookers for corn, two for fish and flesh, and five for butter, cheese, eggs, and poultry, in addition to two regular officers for bread and two for fruits. Ale-tasters there had always been, and leather-searchers, who were required to examine all leather offered for sale and stamp it with a special die, or seal, fixed to the head of a hammer. Woollen cloths were similarly tested and sealed by the aulnager, a royal officer of considerable standing in the Middle Ages. For the purpose of levying tolls, goods had frequently to be valued, and at Manchester, Dr. Tupling tells us,[1] this valuing or appraising, was done by unpaid officers, who were under obligation to buy any goods that remained unsold at the prices fixed, which meant that only tradesmen and merchants of substance could be appointed to the office. It also meant that no market-man could claim that his goods had been over-valued.

The reason for the Town Hall being known as the Tolbooth in so many old towns will already be obvious. It was here that the standard weights and measures were kept, and it is, no doubt, testimony to the importance of the original market-house that so often it did become the civic centre, the place where meetings were held, where the civic regalia was kept, and the headquarters generally of the secular life of the town. Most of these Tolbooths and Moothalls, of which such beautiful examples survive, sometimes surmounted by the market bell, were two-storeyed buildings with the hall, or council chamber, reached by stone steps from the outside.

Most of the grain brought to market was stored at the various inns, a practice called pitching, and only sample bags were shown in the open market for the millers and maltsters to bargain over. Originally the time for this bargaining was afternoon. Later it was brought forward to 11 a.m. in most towns, and it was this earlier starting which introduced that

---

[1] Tupling, *Trans. Lancs and Cheshire Arch. Soc.*, vol. lxviii.

most popular of all market-day institutions, the farmers' ordinary. As soon as the meal was ready the innkeepers came to their doors and rang a bell—a bell as full-throated in its authority as the market bell itself! Immediately, the bargaining stopped, and farmers and millers hurried to their respective inns.

The effect of the development of this country-wide marketing system was revolutionary. Think, for example, of its effect on roads. The great caravans of the fair merchants had travelled along a few ancient tracks, by-passing the towns and leaving their narrow streets to become impassable from the piles of refuse thrown out by slatternly housewives. But when markets were introduced into the settlements themselves, way had to be made for the carriers' carts, which remained such a feature of our country lanes until the slick little vans of the twentieth century rendered them obsolete.

But the vital change was that commerce had now become recognized as the new source of wealth, and treaties for mutual trade were made between towns to such an extent that Southampton, for example, had separate agreements with no fewer than seventy-three corporations, and with all the "honours" in the kingdom, that trading between them should be free from all tolls and customs. In short, the very condition of walled protection that had been so essential when the charters were first granted was now seen to be a barrier that must be broken down wherever possible, and gradually, by removing these obstructions, mutual trust and goodwill between town and town was achieved throughout the kingdom.

For all that, the privileges which burgesses enjoyed in their own markets were jealously guarded. Inhabitants had the privilege of shopping first, and aliens were only admitted into a trading community on payment of a substantial fine. But they were admitted, and it is interesting to note the different names by which they are called in different parts of the kingdom. In the west they were called censers, or chensers, a word that indicates the payment of an annual cense for permission to trade. In the north they were simply called stallingers. In Canterbury they were intrants; in Andover, custumarii, and so forth. Many of them eventually settled in the towns of their choice and established themselves in what appear in municipal records as *shopae* and *seldae*, both of which were originally temporary buildings: the *seldae* what we now call booths, the *shopae* rather more durable single-room sheds or huts, of which the upper half of the front would let down to form an open-air counter and display board.

It is difficult for us to realize how rapid the development of retail trade had been. The now familiar village shop was an unheard of convenience in most parts of the country at the beginning of the nineteenth century. Packmen and pedlars still supplied most of the needs not met by farm or garden between the weekly market or the annual fair, as the case might be. It was only when manufacturing industries were sufficiently developed to displace agricultural workers almost entirely that well-stocked shops for the sale of food came to be looked on as essential—only, that is to say, when the Industrial Revolution was well advanced. Butchers' shops were particularly late. There were none in Oxford, for example, in 1889.[1] Old inadequately ventilated buildings, with small windows, were not suitable places for the storage and display of meat, and the justices had good reason to view them with disfavour, as undoubtedly they did.

When, however, shopkeeping was established throughout the kingdom it largely displaced markets, as in the earlier period markets had displaced fairs. Again the old markets had to be reorganized and in many places re-constituted if they were to survive. By the Local Government Act of 1858 power was conferred on corporate boroughs to establish and control their own markets. The Public Health Act of 1875 extended these powers to Urban District Councils, and that of 1908 to Rural District Councils, subject in each case to the consent of the Minister of Health, who caused a local inquiry to be made before agreeing. Thus we now have our common-law markets—those held either by charter or prescriptive right— and the new statutory markets set up by Act of Parliament. It is still possible for a new market to be set up under charter, but the method may now be considered obsolete, and where the ancient charter market does not meet modern needs a

[1] Report of Royal Commission on Market Rights and Tolls, vol. lv, p. 20.

statutory market can be established in such a way that the two are merged. The large number of auction marts in the country, most of which are privately owned, do not enjoy market protection, and are not in the legal sense markets at all.

And so the traditional English market has receded into the background of the traditional English scene. Much of its appeal to-day is in the heritage of buildings and associations with which it has enriched us. Our great mediæval fairs have left practically nothing behind them. The plough removed every vestige of Sturbridge, the greatest of them all, within a day or two. But markets are an integral part of our lovely old towns, many of which take their name from the old English word "cheaping," corrupted to Chipping. Some of them still have a "Cornmarket," whether used for the sale of corn or not, to remind us that the sale of corn in the market was organized by the lord of the manor's bailiff as early as the end of the twelfth century. And how much of our local history centres in the market cross! The first to be called crosses would be tall shafts raised on steps to give them prominence, but even these were often set up on a boundary stone, and were thus the centre of that neutral ground mentioned in the first chapter. We have an instance of this at Epping.

These market crosses served as symbols of religion, reminding the people of their duty to the Church, a purpose that was pressed home each market day by the preaching friars, and also as points for collecting tolls. The shelter form of cross came in the sixteenth and seventeenth centuries for the most part, and the most beautiful among them were built by the Church—Chichester's by the bishop, Lichfield's by the dean, Abingdon's by the Guild of the Holy Cross. The earliest were octagonal in shape, and were shelters built round the existing cross. In course of time this shelter intended for the monk who was collecting tolls was made large enough to protect the market people, and eventually developed into the great covered-markets of the nineteenth century. Leland, describing the beautiful cross at Malmesbury, says: "There is a right faire and costly piece of worke in the market place, made all of stone, and curiously vaulted, for poor market folks to stand dry when rain cometh. There be eight great pillars and eight open arches, and the work is eight square; one great pillar in the middle beareth up the vault. The men of this towne made this piece of work *in hominum memoriâ.* Malmesbury hath a good quick market, kept every Saturday." The finest of these many beautiful crosses are in the West Country. We think of Salisbury's with its numerous niches and foliated pinnacles, of those at Shepton Mallet, Cheddar, Axbridge, Nether Stowey, and Dunster, of the covered markets at Monmouth, Ross-on-Wye, Chipping Campden, Ludlow, and Shrewsbury, of Dunster's, known to holiday-makers in Somerset, and of those at Amersham in Buckinghamshire and Wallingford in Berkshire. In the north, notwithstanding the greater severity of the weather, they are rare. Middleham in Yorkshire, however, has a remarkable cross in the form of a platform supporting two pillars, one bearing the effigy of a kneeling animal, the other an object traditionally said to be a cheese. Middleham farmers used to observe the true purpose of the cross, which was to symbolize the sacredness of market transactions, by walking up the opposite flights of steps to meet on the cross and there slap hands in concluding the deal. Chichester's is the most beautiful cross in the south, while in the eastern counties, where timber was used, we have such crosses as those at Mildenhall, in Suffolk, and Wymondham and Swaffham in Norfolk.

There is not one of these fine old crosses that is not rich in local if not national associations, or has not echoed with the crying of *Oyez, Oyez, Oyez,* when a public proclamation was about to be made. At Lancaster Charles II was proclaimed in 1651, nine years before he was allowed to rule, and the Pretender proclaimed James III in 1715. The Duke of Monmouth was proclaimed at Bridgwater and Taunton. Banns were called at the market cross in Cromwell's time, and on the bottom step would sit the wrong-doers whose feet were in the stocks. Penance was done here and punishments inflicted. As late as 1822 a poor creature was tied to a cartwheel at Colne Cross in Lancashire and publicly whipped. And, most revolting of all, wives were led to the market-cross with a halter round their necks by their husbands, and sometimes tolls would be collected for these humiliating transactions exactly as when cattle were sold. We remember how Susan Henchard was sold to the highest bidder at Weydon Fair in 1887 as Hardy tells the story in the *Mayor of Caster-bridge*. The latest record of this shameful proceeding in real life is that at Sheffield in 1887, when at the county court a man admitted that some time previously he had bought another man's wife for five shillings.

But these scenes are as well forgotten when we look at these beautiful structures—some in the form of obelisks surmounted by an orb, as at Lavenham and Kirkby Lonsdale, to express the supremacy of the Crown over the Church, some with both orb and cross or rich in ecclesiastical detail.

## CHAPTER V

# London Markets

How the cockney loves and clings to his markets, particularly his street markets! Nothing, it seems, will induce him to part with them or exchange them for cleaner, healthier markets in more convenient places. Their very sites are sacred. And if one is forced to move, as the haymarket was in 1830—when it was transferred to Cumberland Market near Regents Park—the place retains the original name no matter how incongruous it may have become. Reform is regarded as sacrilege. Think, for example, of the imposing Columbia Market, built at immense cost by the Baroness Burdett-Coutts in 1869, so that the people of East London could buy their food in a clean hygienic building instead of in the open street. The experiment failed miserably, as similar if less costly experiments had failed before it. The cockney prefers the rowdy street with its crowd and clatter, where the unexpected may happen—and does happen—at any moment. In a word, the same old London. And can anyone wonder at this when fish has been sold at Billingsgate for a thousand years, poultry at Leadenhall since 1309 or earlier, and when the Rag Fair mentioned

75

by Pope in the *Dunciad*, which was an old-clothes market held in Rosemary Lane, Whitechapel, now Royal Mint Street, still survives?

The one revolutionary change in the Londoner's marketing habits was effected by the Great Fire of 1666, which swept away most of the trading area of the city—the great cheap, or market, which ran between the houses from Tower Street to Newgate, as it had done in Saxon times, and was known as East and West Cheap. The County of London Plan envisaged another great change in 1943, but it has yet to be realized.

In 1930 here were more than ten thousand licensed pitches in the London street markets. Ten years later, however, the Second World War had closed the largest group: those of the great Caledonian Market, the most famous pedlars' market in the world, with up to 2,500 stalls and pitches. But a war cannot kill a market that has outlived many wars. The Caledonian is alive again, though perforce on a different site. And let it be said at once that this amazing bazaar, notwithstanding its name, owes nothing to the Scot. It is rightly claimed as the lineal descendent of the ancient Friday market held on the site of Bartholomew Fair in the days of Rahere, the jester, where it remained until 1855. In that year Smithfield livestock market, which was held on the same site, was transferred to Copenhagen Fields, afterwards Caledonian Road, Islington, and the costermongers followed to claim for themselves "a pitch on the stones," as they called it, with the market whose fortunes they had shared for more than 700 years.

The success of the Caledonian illustrates not only the cockney's refusal to let a market die, but his quickness to seize an opportunity, even though, as in this case, it means changing his line of business. At the time of their removal to Islington the pitchers dealt mainly in old clothes, for which they would scour the country, and, always with an eye for a bargain, at the same time pick up any old junk that seemed likely to yield a few shillings profit. So when a sudden turn of fashion brought antiques into vogue the Caledonian market folk knew exactly where to find them—piled up as they were in attics, servants' quarters, or lumber rooms of country-houses in which Victorian and Edwardian furniture had been

76

displacing them for two generations. In this way the Caledonian costermongers came to run a trade in antiques that was the envy of established dealers with generations of accumulated knowledge behind their businesses. Society ladies, well-known actresses, and American collectors of every kind of rarity visited the Caledonian and boasted of bargains picked up on the stones. It is admitted that a few experienced connoisseurs came in to share this amazing success; but at least three out of five of the traders were members of old market families, many of whom—the "Silver Kings" most notably—became knowledgeable, and indeed came to be recognized as experts.

There was a rakish atmosphere about the place that appealed to the bargain hunters, although most of the traders were respectable enough, and not a few of them well-to-do. It is true, as was always alleged, that a certain amount of stolen property was disposed of by a few cheap-jacks, of a race still to be met with in some of the London street markets, one of which is even known as "Loot Alley." Among these, low whistles are sometimes heard passing along the street to warn confederates that "the coppers" are about.

At the end of the war the Caledonian pitchers were refused permission to return, and although in 1949 13,500 persons signed a petition supporting them, the Court of Common Council decided against reopening. In 1950, therefore, a new site was found at the meeting of Bermondsey Street and Tower Bridge Road, where about two hundred stalls carry on the same old business in antiques, knick-knacks, and curios every Tuesday and Friday. But there is none of the old excitement. The dealers, all by now experts in their special lines, usually arrive in their cars and hire the stalls, although there are a few who pitch in the old way. Whether the number will grow or not remains to be seen. Most of them belong to the old families, and in spite of their prosperity have the same old coster spirit. They are part of a London that can neither be killed by adversity nor spoiled by prosperity.

This immemorial world of the costermonger has its outcrops north, south, east, and west in London, which are like those wild flowers of the field that the gardener can never finally eradicate from his sophisticated beds and borders.

And why should they be rooted out? The drab streets they bring such colour and life to are theirs by right. What will astonish the inquiring visitor in all of them is the long pedigree of trading many of the stallholders can claim. But this other world of the London street markets is full of surprises. Who, for example, would suspect that within a stone's throw of Piccadilly Circus survive coster markets that might have come straight out of Dickens or Mayhew? Yet there they are —in Berwick Street and Rupert Street. And the same incongruity is to be experienced in Leather Lane, at the lunch-hour market behind Gamage's store in Holborn where the office boys pick up their wireless parts and odds and ends of electrical equipment. In Stow's day Leather Lane ran through an impoverished district "infested with thieves and beggars," and was itself "narrow and dirty, lined with stalls and barrows and itinerant dealers in fish, bacon, vegetables, plasterers' or image shops, and old clothes." The Leather Lane of to-day is the lineal descendant of this and survives in spite of the modernization about it. Even nearby Farringdon Street retains its barrows of old books and prints which the man with an hour to spare can turn over to his heart's content, then buy for a few coppers something he will own with pleasure for the rest of his life. If that is not value, what is?

Mayhew knew these markets well. In his day there were fifteen of them held on Sunday mornings. "The most crowded of these," he says, "are held in that part of Lambeth called the New Cut and in that part of Somers Town known as 'The Brill.' These are both half a mile in length, and each of them is frequented by as nearly as possible three hundred hucksters." The Brill has gone, but the hucksters have moved into neighbouring streets, where it is still "Business as Usual" with them.

But what would Mayhew say of Petticoat Lane to-day? Perhaps the first thing for anyone to say is that until you see it you cannot believe anything so thrilling could be maintained Sunday by Sunday year in and year out. It has the kind of excitement most towns whip up for a memorable celebration, and a few for an annual fête; but to draw such crowds weekly, and to sustain such exuberance hour after hour requires stamina, verbosity, and a faculty for self-intoxication beyond the capacity of most. With their wares spread round them, a fancy hat set at an angle on their head, shirt sleeves rolled up and eyes shining with excitement, the champions of Petticoat Lane hold their crowds spellbound with a torrent of sales talk until suddenly the moment arrives for mysterious crates to be ripped open, and attendants to rush forward shouting "Ten bob a time, ten bob a time. Two of 'em, thankee kindly, lidy, ten bob a time." And the ten-shilling and pound notes are picked up as easily, apparently, and certainly as snappily, as sparrows pick up crumbs, while the great man mops his brow in preparation for his next terrific onslaught. And when you learn that there are up to 1,000 of these hucksters, all trying to shout each other down and hold for a few seconds a crowd that one could only compare with that of a London tube-station during the daily rush hour, surprise gives place to bewilderment. That thousands should come up at week-ends for the kind of punishment they endure daily would pass belief if it were not that these Petticoat Lane hucksters are such masters of their craft. Here, for example, in Lord Mayor's hat and robes, is their leader, Mike Stern, president for a generation of the Stepney Street Traders' Association, the Shakespearean draper who scorns the smart patter of lesser mortals and from his stall in Harrow Place declaims such noble periods as: "Oh, when I am dead and forgotten, as I shall be, and sleep in dull, cold marble with . . ."—then, having transfixed his audience, springs forward with: "these lovely utility towels, ten bob a pair, ten bob a pair."

For the rest of the week Petticoat Lane is Middlesex Street, the name it was given in 1830, and is lined with shops that are neither more nor less exciting than hundreds of others in the vicinity. It sprawls, however, into Wentworth and Goulston Streets.

In Stow's time it was Hog Lane, a genuine country lane pleasantly bordered with hedgerows and noble elms, "insomuch," says Stow, "that some gentlemen of the Court and City built their houses here for air." Gondomar, the Spanish ambassador was one, and Hans Jacobson, jeweller to James I, had "a fair and large house" in the neighbourhood. It was probably on account of these connections that the name was discarded and Petticoat Lane adopted instead. Anyhow, it appears as "Peticote Lane" on Rythers map of 1608, and in 1616 Ben Jonson wrote:

> We will survey the suburbs and make forth our salleys,
> Down Petticoat Lane and up the smock alleys.

Nothing of these proud associations is left now. No doubt these well-to-do residents fled at the time of the Plague, leaving the lane to become a derelict area until refugees from religious persecution on the Continent—to be mentioned presently in connection with Spitalfields—settled here and gave it the trading reputation it has been developing ever since. Petticoat Lane is thus different from the smaller street markets in that it has this foreign element about it, intermingled with the irrepressible cockney.

There is no historical significance in the fact, but in view of what was said in the first chapter it is interesting to note that Middlesex Street forms the boundary between Stepney and London, so that one side is patrolled by the City police, the other by the Metropolitan, which at one time meant that what happened in the middle of the street was nobody's business. To-day, however, the Stepney Traders' Association are so jealous of their street's good name that any irregularities are quickly checked. With as many as 100,000 potential customers passing along the street on a Sunday morning their goodwill is too valuable an asset to take risks with, particularly after the fight they put up a few years ago to save it.

In the early years of the present century the hucksters used to fight each other for the best pitches, so that for an hour or more the place would be pandemonium. Then in 1928 the Stepney Borough Council intervened under the provisions of the L.C.C. General Powers Act and succeeded in regulating the market by licensing the traders. Nevertheless numerous attempts were made to abolish it altogether. Buses and fire-engines were driven through the crowds; petitions were got up to abolish Sunday trading altogether. But the market won, and in 1936 Sunday trading was legalized by Act of Parliament. Since then Petticoat Lane has become a national institution, and with such picturesque characters as

Ras Prince Monolulu, the tipster, to be met there it has become one of the recognized sights of London.

Other street markets in the neighbourhood are the Club Row pets' market and the bird market in Sclater Street. Elsewhere are the Sunday street markets of Brixton, Lambeth Walk, Mile End Waste, the New Cut, and scores of others, in any of which we are again in touch with the immemorial London that retains its own cheeky, witty, buoyant, and good humoured identity in spite of the overshadowing Metropolis, as surely as the old towns of Yorkshire and Devon retain theirs.

Meanwhile the five greater markets, the chartered markets of Billingsgate, Smithfield, Leadenhall, Spitalfields, and Covent Garden, have outgrown their cockneydom, and have become national markets, cutting themselves adrift, as it were, from their own traditions. Nevertheless Billingsgate, Smithfield, and Leadenhall are essentially people's markets, with rights based on the Edward III charter which gave the city sole rights within 7 miles of London Stone, although somewhat perversely we find that these are now wholesale markets almost exclusively, while the retail markets, with the notable exception of two in Woolwich, are for the most part privately owned. The city rights, however, were set at nought by Charles II, who granted charters for both Spitalfields and Covent Garden, while other markets appear to have sprung up spontaneously in a way that would never have been tolerated elsewhere—the Pudding Lane fruit market, for example, which survived until 1929. Outside the city this natural tolerance of the Londoner has been curiously restrained, with the result that not one of the twenty-eight boroughs of Greater London, with the single exception of Woolwich, owns a market. Nor does the London County Council own markets, although in 1882 the Duke of Bedford did enter into negotiations with the Metropolitan Board of Works, the forerunner of the London County Council, for the sale of Covent Garden. So when people from the industrial areas of the Midlands and North move into London they are surprised to find none of the great market halls they are accustomed to shop in. Instead they find more than a hundred of these small unchartered street markets, which only the sentimental cockney would tolerate to-day.

# London Markets

As London's street markets can give, if only for a moment, the illusion of an old-fashioned country town, Billingsgate, situated on Thames bank between London Bridge and the Tower, might still be the sea-washed quay of a fishing town, although in point of fact practically all its fish comes by road or rail now. To see it at the top of its form you must be there at 6 a.m.; but unless you are as tough as the Billingsgate porters themselves you will be well advised to stay by the Monument. From there you can watch these white-coated porters, who wear the famous low-crowned leather hats studded with brass nails, which are said to have descended directly from the helmets worn by the bowmen at Agincourt —carry piles of crates on their heads. I am told that once a porter's neck sets it will bear a weight greater than that of his body. To-day, in fact, his neck is much stronger than his language!

No one, apparently, knows how Billingsgate gained its reputation for foul, abusive language; but I was assured that it went out with the fishwives. I can well believe it. No doubt it also came in with them. The word is defined in old dictionaries as the language of "a scolding, impudent slut," and in *The Chronicle History of King Lear*, the Messenger, in reply to Goneril's commendation of his "good tongue," says: "And as bad a tongue, if it be set on, as any oyster-wife at Billingsgate hath." With her basket before her, a clay pipe in her mouth, and a bottle of gin at her side, she was one of the less reputable London characters for centuries. Rowlandson has her in his *Microcosm of London*.

That the old-time porters should have inherited the fishwives' reputation was particularly unjust because traditionally they were a most respectable body of men, most of whom, as members of an ancient gild, were freemen of the City of London. There were four classes of them—market, fellowship, tackle, and company's porters, all men of substance who attended an annual service in St. Mary-at-Hill, at which they handed to the clergy a generous subscription for local charities. Although much of its original purpose was lost, this Billingsgate Porters' gild survived until its remaining functions were

taken over by the Dockers' Union in 1894. The reason for the exceptional status of Billingsgate porters in those days was the great responsibility of the post before the London docks were constructed. It was then the custom for all vessels entering the port to unload into lighters while still in midstream, which meant that dishonest men could sink boxes of fish at the time, to be recovered and turned into cash later. The men handling such cargoes had, therefore, to be above suspicion. In short, the porter's was a position of trust.

The name of the market is said to be a corruption of Belin's Gate. Geoffrey of Monmouth's story is that at this point one Belin, or Belinus, a legendary British king of the fifth century B.C., cut a hythe in the river bank, and set up a quay of poles and planks alongside it. No doubt the place does take its name from a person, though not a king, and no doubt its date is later than that ascribed to it by Geoffrey of Monmouth. It is now thought to have been one of the two river gates of the Roman city.

Whatever its early history may have been, Billingsgate was an obvious place for a market to develop long before there was any question of a charter, although its supremacy did not, in fact, remain unchallenged. In the thirteenth century it had to cope with the rivalry of Queenhithe, the customs of which, as the name implies, went to the Queen, and to make sure that these should be adequate Henry III commanded the constables of the Tower of London to order all ships coming from the Cinque Ports to land their cargoes at the Queen's quay. Nevertheless the older port survived, and in Stow's time all kinds of produce were landed at Billingsgate, although fish was already the staple, as some of the neighbouring streets bear testimony. Stow tells us that the houses then occupied by Billingsgate fishmongers "were at first but moveable boards or stalls, set out on market-days, to strew their fish there to be sold; but, procuring license to set up sheds, they grew to shops, and little by little to tall houses, of three or four storeys in height, and are now called Fish Street."

An Act passed in 1559 limited the commodities to be sold at Billingsgate, and by a statute of 1699 it was finally established by William III, its most generous patron, as a free and open market for fish. One of its most interesting privileges is that enjoyed by William's own countrymen for the sale of live eels. Their boats are still to be seen moored off the wharf. In fact they never leave, because tradition has it that in order to keep the privilege there must always be one Dutch eel boat at Billingsgate. For this reason the present boat must never cast its moorings until another has come in to take its place. Traditions and legends, however, are for curious visitors. Billingsgate finds the selling of fish a full-time job, and well it might, for crates come in daily from fishing grounds extending from the Dogger Bank to the Arctic Circle. It would be difficult to find a single fishing town in the United Kingdom that does not send most of its catch to Billingsgate, from there to be distributed throughout the land again. Six hundred tons, approximately, are handled daily in buildings erected in 1877 to a design by Sir Horace Jones, the city architect, who was responsible for the nearby Tower Bridge, which, incidentally, so enraged H. G. Wells.

## THE BOROUGH

Borough Market, Southwark, traditionally the poor man's fruit and vegetable market, may be at least as old as Billingsgate. No one knows. Undoubtedly it goes back well into the time when the Thames was the southern boundary of London. But while its origin must remain speculative its development was probably due to the narrow streets of the old city becoming too congested for the fruit growers south of the river to find room in them. Little is heard of it before 1276; but it may well have been there when the Roman legions advanced on London through Kent.

Its charter, granted by Edward VI and confirmed by Charles II in 1671, was for a market in the street; but by the 1750s this had come to be regarded as an intolerable nuisance, and an Act of 1757 decreed that it should be abolished on its old site and reconstituted in Rochester Yard, a site provided by the Court of Common Council, where it has remained ever since. At first the new site pleased no one except the Council. It was unpopular with the buyers and it was too expensive for the sellers. Consequently the market

declined to insignificant proportions until the coming of the
railway enabled large supplies to be brought in from all the
southern counties, and the Borough was restored to its
rightful place as one of London's greater markets. It is now
managed for the benefit of the ratepayers by twenty-one
trustees appointed by the Southwark council on the nomina-
tion of the councillors of St. Saviour's Ward.

Smithfield is now the dead-meat market. Traditionally it
was the great livestock market, which in England means
more than the visitor from overseas may realize. To appreciate
its importance we have to cast our minds back to the palmy
days of the Smithfield Club, when the English took more
pride in their cattle shows than in anything else, with the
possible exception of the Derby. The nobility and gentry of
those days, after giving their minds in the middle of the
eighteenth century to the building of their stately houses,
and the laying out of their parks and gardens, were following
the example of their young king, who was to ripen into
"Farmer George," and throwing themselves heart and soul
into the mysteries of cattle breeding. It was in this world
that the Smithfield Club became charged with the authority
of what for a time was almost a cult. At its meetings you
might meet a royal duke discussing with a stout yeoman the
values of sliced turnips and mangold-worzel for the production of beef, milk, or whatever it is that mangold-worzel does
produce! The bluffness of the stockyard and the country
market, rather than the elegance that had gone with the
Adam interior and the Capability Brown landscape, had
become the sign of the confident well-born Englishman.

But Smithfield was much older than the fashion. Like the
beasts that were sold there the market had a pedigree. We
have already referred to it in writing of Bartholomew Fair,
its near neighbour. Here was held the famous Friday market
mentioned a moment ago, at which as early as Henry II's
time the noblemen of the day bought their mounts—and
bought them as horses are still bought at Barnet and the
many horse fairs of the north of England, after seeing them

trotted briskly up and down the field to show off their paces. William Fitzstephen, the first historian of London, has a vivid description of the scene: "On this side are the horses most fit for esquires, moving with harder pace yet swiftly, that lift and set down together, as it were, the opposite fore and hind feet; on that side colts of fine breed who, not yet well used to the bit,

*Altius incedunt, et mollia crura reponunt* [1]

In that part are the sumpter horses, powerful and spirited; here costly chargers elegant of form, noble of stature, with ears quickly tremulous, necks lifted, haunches plump. . . . In another part of the field stand by themselves the goods proper to rustics, implements of husbandry, swine with long flanks, cows with full udders, oxen of bulk immense, and woolly flocks. There stand the mares fit for plough, dray and cart, some big with foal, and others with their young colts closely following." This same Smithfield was the favourite place for jousts and tournaments. Stow tells us that "In 1357 great and royal jousts were holden in Smithfield; there being present the Kings of England, France, and Scotland, with many other nobles and great estates of divers lands." But Smithfield to-day is a meat market, and these flights of the winged steed are no longer appropriate.

From 1150 to 1850 the old Smithfield market served London and the surrounding country as a livestock market. And even at the end of that long period, when the driving of cattle through miles of London streets had become brutal and in every way intolerable, its removal was fiercely opposed. But the City Corporation was determined, and after prolonged negotiations it was transferred to Islington in 1855. In its place was erected the present London Central Markets, with their thirty entrance gates, their towers and domes, built to Sir Horace Jones's design and opened as the new Smithfield Market in 1868.

### SPITALFIELDS

On Spitalfields, as on Smithfield, £2,000,000 was expended in erecting a thoroughly efficient and workmanlike place of

[1] 'Prance high, and rear their supple necks,' from Virgil's *Georgics*.

business; but with both, except for those who have business to do in them, their interest is in their past rather than in their present.

Spitalfields is held by right of a charter granted by Charles II to a certain John Balch and his heirs for a market in the vicinity of Spital Square. These rights were acquired by the City Corporation in the present century and the building of the new premises, with 6 acres under glass and 1½ miles of warehouses, was authorized in 1922. So much for the facts; but to those of us who have neither buying nor selling to do there, Spitalfields must always be the place where the Protestant weavers settled after the revocation of the Edict of Nantes in 1685. The story is well known. Louis XIV had married Madame de Maintenon, his mistress, the previous year, and under her influence the gaiety of an enlightened court had given place to religious gloom as the king fell under the spell of his queen and her Church. Gradually the privileges enjoyed by the French Huguenots were reduced until in 1685 the final and disastrous step of revoking the Edict was taken. But it was to be a step of great benefit to England, when, under the Protestant rule of William III, these persecuted folk were brought over and allowed to build their houses and ply their trade of silk-weaving in the derelict area of Spitalfields, to which they brought such wealth that they became known as "the profitable strangers."

### LEADENHALL

Not far away, at what is now merely the corner of Gracechurch street, but in Roman times was the crossing of the east–west thoroughfares of the city, is Leadenhall, yet another market rebuilt by Sir Horace Jones, the city architect, and now famous for its Christmas shows of game and poultry. Leadenhall, however, brings the country to the town at any time of the year, and has more of the character of the old-time market—the people's market—than any other in London. It takes its name, we are told, from the house of a certain Sir Hugh Neville who lived there in the fourteenth century and was allowed to hold a market for the benefit of his tenants; but it is to two lord mayors that it owes its traditional status.

The first of these was Dick Whittington himself, through whose endeavours the Corporation acquired the manor early in the fifteenth century. The second was Sir Simon Eyre, 1445–6, who converted the lead-roofed mansion of the Nevilles into a storehouse for provisions against a time of famine in the city. This forethought was repaid in 1512, when, as Stow relates, famine did come to London, and the Lord Mayor of that year drove to Leadenhall early in the morning in order to supervise the distribution of food from Sir Simon Eyre's huge granary.

For an idea of what Leadenhall represented in Stuart London we recall the remark of the Spanish ambassador, Don Petro de Rouquillo, who in passing this way in the company of Charles II exclaimed: "There is more meat sold in your market than in all the kingdom of Spain." As Penant, who wrote an account of London in 1790, says: "Leadenhall market is a wonder to foreigners, who do not duly consider the carnivorous nation to which it belongs."

## COVENT GARDEN

Undoubtedly the market dearest to the English heart is Covent Garden, where "Cabbages and Kings" really are associated, and with them music and all the arts. The belief that a convent stood on the site is without foundation. The origin of this error was a misunderstanding of the connection of the site with the Abbey of Westminster, which had a "pleasant garden" hereabouts, used as a burial ground. At the Dissolution the abbey garden passed to John, Earl of Bedford, and became the centre of a new and fashionable quarter for which Inigo Jones built the church that was to have more celebrities buried in its vaults than any other except the abbey and the cathedrals—the church in which Dr. Johnson worshipped, and which was eventually to be known as "the actors' church." Shaw's *Pygmalion* was filmed on its Tuscan portico, which once overlooked the piazza: inspired, it is said, by the one at Leghorn, as the piazza at Covent Garden in turn inspired the London squares.

The market itself is believed to have sprung up sponta-

neously with the fruit- and flower-sellers who, incidentally, wore the becoming Ranelagh caps—making use of the open space so conveniently sheltered by the arcades of Ben Jonson's piazza. The Earl of Bedford, whose gardens adjoined, built a shelter for them in 1632, and thirty-eight years later was granted letters patent authorizing this now established market in "a place commonly called the Piazza," near the church of St. Paul, Covent Garden. In consideration of this grant the earl undertook to spend a large sum in remedying "the confusion and inconvenience then existing"; but the market became so popular that improvements never have kept pace with expansion.

The present market was designed by Charles Fowler for the Duke of Bedford in 1828, and though it has been sadly despoiled since then, it still has the dignity and charm which the more efficiently planned markets east of it lack. Quite apart from the growth of London, no one in 1830 could have foreseen how popular fruit would become in the twentieth century, nor that the speeding up of transport would make it possible to bring fruit and flowers from such distances and yet offer them as fresh as if they had been picked the same morning in one's own garden. So it is no wonder that, notwithstanding the boldness of the Floral Hall at the time it was built in 1860, the 1872 market fronting on to Wellington Street, and the extensions of 1887 and 1890, the market has burst its bounds time after time, until the confusion has become unbelievable—although the market people themselves will assure you that there is none!

Covent Garden's association with the stage began in 1732 with the opening of the Covent Garden Theatre, built on the authority of letters patent granted long before that by Charles II to Sir William Davenant "to build a theatre in London, Westminster, or the suburbs thereof, wherein tragedies, comedies, plays, operas, musick, scenes, and all other entertainments of the stage whatsoever, may be shown and presented." Of this earlier Covent Garden we have records in old prints, showing the square with steps for the flower-girls and a fluted column to represent a market cross. The heyday of its social life was under the first two Georges, when all the great ones of the day—Addison, Pope, Fielding,

Wilkes, Garrick, and Hogarth—frequented its coffee-houses and disported themselves in the piazza.

How long it will remain on its present site is an open question. Hitherto all attempts to move it have failed. The 1943 County of London plan provides for its removal to a site at King's Cross; but whether the trading goes elsewhere or not, Covent Garden will always be associated in the minds of most of us with the great ones who lived there—with Sir Godfrey Kneller, Sir Peter Lely, Zoffany, and Lady Mary Wortley Montagu—and with the coffee-houses—Will's and Button's—which drew to the place all the wits and poets of Augustan England. And if it is objected that these are not market but literary associations, the answer is that when the traditional fairs and markets flourished the poet and the pedlar, the player and the flower-girl mingled together as happily in the heart of London as they still do for a few brief hours, if only in masquerade, at an annual village fair.

THE FLORAL HALL, COVENT GARDEN

## CHAPTER VI

# The Fun o' the Fair

No one knows better than the cockney how to enjoy himself, and if he learnt the art anywhere he learnt it at the old London fairs. Besides St. Bartholomew's there was St. Edward's Fair at Westminster, sometimes called Magdalen's, which was originally held in St. Margaret's churchyard and afterwards in Tothill Fields; and Southwark, or Lady Fair, depicted by Hogarth and visited by both Pepys and Evelyn. But the Londoner has been much less successful in keeping his fairs than in keeping his markets. Lady Fair was suppressed in 1762; Magdalen in the nineteenth century.

Among the wonders of Lady Fair were the monkeys and apes dancing on tight ropes, described by Evelyn, the tricks of an Italian wench, whom all the Court went to see, and the puppet shows that Pepys chuckled over so much—"And how that idle thing do work upon people that see it, and even myself too!" For riotous abandonment it rivalled even "old Bartlemy." In his fable of the two monkeys Gay relates that here,

The tumbler whirles the flip-flap round,
With summersets he shakes the ground;
The cord beneath the dancer springs;
Aloft in air the vaulter swings,
Distorted now, now prone depends,
Now through his twisted arms ascends;
The crowd in wonder and delight,
With clapping hands applaud the sight.

A third once popular London fair, St. James's, granted by
Edward I to the hospital "for maidens that are leprous,"
which stood where Henry VIII built the palace of that name,
was the subject of an amusing entry in Machyn's diary on
the 25th June, 1560. "St. James fayer by Westminster was
so great that a man could not have a pygg for money; and
the bear wiffes had nother meate nor drink before iiij of cloke
in the same day. And the chese went very well away for 1*d*.
q. the pounde. Besides the great and mighti armie of beggares
and bandes that were there."

Tower Hill had another now forgotten fair, granted by
Edward III to "the master, brothers, chaplain, and sisters of
St. Katherine's, to be held upon the King's ground in all places
thereof, opposite to the Abbey of Graces, next the Tower."
Several such fairs have gone without leaving a trace behind
them beyond the mere record of their grant; but one London
fair, that on the east side of Hyde Park, will be perpetuated
because its name has been assumed by London's most
fashionable quarter. Mayfair reached its zenith later than the
others, and may indeed have owed much of its success to
their suppression. It was granted by James II in 1689 for
"the buying and selling of all manner of goods and merchandises" and must have been immensely popular, because
on the 27th April, 1700, the London newspapers announced
that, "In Brookfield Market Place, at the east corner of
Hyde Park, is a fair to be kept for the space of sixteen days,
beginning with the 1st of May; the first three days for live
cattle and leather, with the same entertainments as at Bartholomew Fair; where there are shops to be let ready built
for all manner of tradesmen that usually keep fairs, and so to
continue yearly at the same place." It is clear that the buying
and selling of merchandise had already ceased to be the major

attraction and that Mayfair had become, in fact, a second Bartholomew's.

The original nucleus of Mayfair was a two-storeyed market house, with butchers' and poulterers' shops on the ground floor, and the usual chamber above, which at fair time was let as a theatre. Around it spread the now familiar attractions: stalls for gingerbread-sellers and booths for jugglers and prize-fighters—both at cudgels and back-sword. There were boxing matches, wild beast shows, fire-eaters, eel-divers, bull-baiters, hasty-pudding eaters, as well as the inevitable merry-go-rounds and such competitions as grinning for a hat and running for a shift. The Ducking Pond became the chief attraction. This sport, which remained so popular from the time of Charles II to the time of George IV and even later, was a duck-hunt. The duck was placed on the pond, and a number of small dogs were sent after it. The fun arose from the dexterity of the duck in diving under water whenever a dog came near, until finally one, more cunning than the rest, won the contest by catching her. A 1748 handbill will give an idea of the sporting instincts aroused:

"At Mayfair ducking pond, on Monday next, the 27th of June, Mr. Hooton's dog (with hardly a tooth in his head to hold a duck, but well known by his goodness to all that have seen him hunt), hunts six ducks for a guinea against the bitch called Flying Spaniel, from the ducking pond on the other side of the water, who has beaten all she has hunted against except Mr. Hooton's Good Blood."

Another favourite diversion at Mayfair was the witnessing of mock executions, which by either representing or referring to that of Lord Lovat roused fierce political feelings and often resulted in free fights.

The personality of the fair was a gingerbread-vendor named Tiddy-Doll, a typical fair-ground character matched in our own day by Ras Prince Monolulu. Tiddy-Doll was a dandy. His favourite costume was a white suit trimmed with gold lace, which he wore with a lace-ruffed shirt, a laced hat adorned with a feather, white silk stockings, and, when selling his gingerbread, a fine white apron. He appears in a characteristic pose with a gingerbread cake in his left hand in Hogarth's execution of the "Idle Prentice at Tyburn."

Mayfair seems to have been regarded as a public nuisance almost from the start; but when the constables of St. Martin's tried to close it in 1702 they were so violently set upon by about thirty persons with drawn swords, and a mob armed with sticks and stones, that one of the constables was killed. A fencing-master named Cooke was executed for the crime. In 1708 the fair was presented as a nuisance by the Grand Jury of Westminster, and either lapsed or was suppressed for a time; but it sprang to life again and survived until 1764, when its final suppression appears to have been the result of complaints by Lord Coventry, who had a house in Piccadilly and not unnaturally found its rowdiness insufferable.

When the West End began to take its vices more quietly the rowdies moved east and for a few years Bow Fair provided an outlet for high spirits until in 1822 that also was suppressed. To Bow Fair, according to an old song, the people thronged from all quarters:

> The waterman with Wapping whores
> Over the fields do comes by scores.

They were joined at the fair by Spitalfields weavers and heaven knows who else. When complaints were made about this particular fair no charter could be found for it, and the submission that it was by prescription because it had been held from time immemorial was not accepted by the bench. Thus Bow Fair was suppressed without difficulty and something of the reaction of the people to the closing of this and similar spurious, or customary, fairs is to be learned from a long *Elegy on the Death of Bow Fair*, of which a few of the verses run:

> No more shall cockneys don their Sunday coats,
> Stepney, Brook-green, or brighter Bow to fill;
> No folk shall row to Greenwich hill in boats,
> And roll in couples down One Tree Hill!
>
> Girls shall no longer dance in gingham gowns,
> Nor monkeys sit on organs at the door;
> Gongs shall be turn'd to frying pans; and Clowns
> Take to the country and be clowns no more.

## Southwark Fair

No learned-pig, no veal, no muttom pie.
No heads be crack'd, no undergarments won.
No giants twelve, no dwarfs just three-feet high.
No calves with two heads shown to calves with one. . . .

The magistrates decree that "fair is foul,"
And put a stop to profitable sport;
They exorcise the Lion's shilling howl,
And cut the Irish giant's income short. . . .

Take warning, then, ye fair! from this fair's fall!
One Act—the vagrant Act—hath been its ruin.
Listen, oh listen, to Law's *Serious Call*,
For fun and pleasure lead but to undoing!

The liveliest time in the genuine London fairs came, as we should expect, at the Restoration as a reaction from the austerity of the Commonwealth, during which players and showmen had been dispersed throughout the country to earn a precarious living by secret performances in lonely barns, or at country fairs, in the Catholic north and west. The announcement of the arrival of Charles II in May 1660 was the best news they had heard for nearly twenty years. It brought all who were still active enough back to the capital at the double. So on the 13th September of that year we find Evelyn noting that he had seen monkeys and apes dancing on the tight rope at St. Margaret's Fair in Southwark, that "they were gallantly clad *à la mode*, went upright, saluted the company, bowing and pulling off their hats; they saluted one another with as good a grace as if instructed by a dancing master; they turned heels over head with a basket having eggs in it, without breaking any." But of Southwark Fair, it was Hogarth, of course, who produced the enduring and inimitable record, introducing every showman and fairground character of the day into it. The person vaulting the rope is an Italian named Volante, a renowned acrobat of George I's time; The giant Maximilian is there, exhibited on a showcloth. He was from Saxony. The acrobat, Cadman, who broke his neck at Shrewsbury in 1740,[1] is depicted in a daring leap from a church tower, and all in all no better portrayal of the fair could either be desired or imagined.

[1] *The Gentleman's Magazine*, February, 1740.

## The Fun o' the Fair

The continuing prosperity of fairs in seventeenth- and eighteenth-century London is shown in the spontaneous "frost fairs" of which there are so many accounts that little need be said about them here. Evelyn's is perhaps the best account of the one which sprang up during the Great Frost of 1683–4, which he summed up as "a bacchanalian triumph, or carnival on the water." So thick was the ice that an ox was roasted whole on the river near Whitehall. These, however, were no more fairs in the true sense than the jollifications held to celebrate such rare events as a Coronation or a Declaration of Peace are fairs.

Meanwhile both regular and irregular fairs were being steadily pushed from the centre outwards as London grew and the open spaces were built over. Greenwich and Stepney were the most popular at one time. Others—Croydon's for example—came to the fore later when railways extended the range of pleasure as well as the range of boredom, until towards the end of the nineteenth century London was encircled by these country fairs, some of which were, in fact, ancient charter fairs made popular by easier transport. Ealing, Mitcham, Camberwell, Enfield, come to mind as examples. Most of them were regarded by the magistrates as nuisances, and sooner or later most of those without charters were suppressed. Yet such was the popularity of these country fairs round London that to suppress them in one place led inevitably to an outbreak elsewhere, and often where control was more difficult. As the legal adviser to the City Corporation had said in the 1730s, "It is at all times difficult by law to put down the ancient customs and practices of the multitude."

The most popular of these spurious fairs south of the river was the Easter and Whitsuntide fair at Greenwich, for which from crack of dawn the river and the old Kent Road were alive with excited crowds in wherries and waggonettes, pouring out eastwards to the park in which booths and stalls were set up on the greensward where queens and their ladies had once disported themselves. The hill was the focal point, and was the scene of the game that is particularly associated with Greenwich Fair, that of chasing or pulling partners down the slope mentioned a moment ago in the *Elegy on the Death of Bow Fair*. Meanwhile people climbed the hill to join the

crowd that had gathered round several merry old pensioners who offered the use of their telescopes at a halfpenny a time to enable their clients to see the pirates hanging in chains along the opposite bank of the river.

The scene at Greenwich can never be lost since it is described by Dickens in *Sketches by Boz*. "Imagine yourself," he says, "in an immensely dense crowd which swings you to and fro and in and out, and every way but the right one; add to this the screams of women, the shouts of boys, the clanging of gongs, the firing of pistols, the ringing of bells, the bellowing of speaking-trumpets, the squeaking of penny dittoes, the noise of a dozen bands with three drums in each, all playing different tunes at the same time, the hallooing of showmen, and an occasional roar from the wild beast shows; and you are in the very centre and heart of the fair.

"This immense booth, with the large stage in front, so brightly illuminated with variegated lamps and pots of burning fat, is 'Richardson's,' where you have a melodrama (with three murders and a ghost), a pantomime, a comic song, an overture, and some incidental music, all done in five-and-twenty minutes. The company are now promenading outside in all the dignity of wigs, spangles, red ochre, and whitening. . . . The exhibitions next in popularity to these itinerant theatres are the travelling menageries, or, to speak more intelligibly, the 'wild beast shows,' where a military band in beef-eaters costume, with leopard-skin caps, plays incessantly, and where large highly coloured representations of tigers tearing men's heads open, and a lion being burnt with red hot irons to induce him to drop his victim, are hung up outside, by way of attracting visitors."

Richardson's [1] drew the biggest crowds. In fact to most people Greenwich was now before everything else the place for circuses and wild beast shows—Richardson's from about 1804 and Wombwell's Royal Menagerie from about 1820, while among smaller shows were those of Clarke, Samwell, Cooke, Saunders, and Batty. No one, apparently, knows

---

[1] John Richardson (1767?–1837) was born in a workhouse at Great Marlow. He joined a travelling company as a boy. In 1796 he became licensee of "The Harlequin," a public-house opposite the stage-door of Drury Lane, and gave performances there before taking to the road with his own travelling company.

when the fair began. It would be a small local affair at first; but by 1761, according to a correspondent in *Lloyd's Evening Post* on the 24th March of that year, the number attending on Easter Monday was estimated at 15,000, which means that it was already more than a local event. Its greatest popularity came between 1835 and 1860 when its booths and stalls spread through all the principal streets of the town. So popular had it become that in 1838 it was estimated that 200,000 persons attended the Easter fair. Such crowds would always slip the leash by nightfall, when the drink began to work in them, and no one was surprised, therefore, when at the Easter fair in 1850 there was rioting and wholesale destruction of property. After that the suppression of the fair was certain.

Spurious as it was, Greenwich is important in the history of fairs because here, at the Easter fair of 1835, the roundabout was introduced to the British public. Writing of the innovation, a contemporary newspaper reports[1]:

"The principal object of attraction at this Scene of Fun and Frolick, was a Mechanical Machine, or Round About. Its construction for the purpose was entirely novel, consisting of a large mast in the centre of a frame of strong timber; and at nearly the summit were two cross beams which were attached by a bolt passing through the centre of each of them on different levels; at the four ends of these were suspended a model of a brig full rigged, about the size of a wherry; these were hung by iron bars, and contained seats for four persons. The method of putting them in motion was beneath, by two men turning a wheel; and, connected with each cross-arm above, was an upright which moved on two circular stages, similar to the inclined plane upon which the moon of an orrery moves, and having a loose joint gave the beams an ascending and descending motion, as a see-saw, as well as of a circular movement. The whole of the machinery was concealed from the publick by a pyramidal octagon enclosure."

At the same time advertisements appeared offering this "singular invention" for hire:

"To The Proprietors of Public Gardens, &c. The 'Voyage

[1] British Museum, Fillinham Collection of Cuttings.

Volante,' or, a Sail in the Air, from the Champs Elysee, Paris, will be introduced into England for the first time on Monday next, and will be erected on the Fair Ground at Greenwich, merely for the observance of those who may wish to treat for the hire of the same. Besides the daily recreation which it affords in the sensation of Flying, which it gives, it is capable of performing numerous night spectacles, and calculated, by night and day, to attract in England as it has done in Paris." The showmen had to wait another forty years or so before pony or manual power was superseded by steam.

In public scandal Greenwich was outdone for a time by its neighbour, Charlton—not surprisingly in view of the reputed origin of this notorious Horn Fair! According to the legend, King John, while hunting over Shooters Hill and Blackheath from his palace at Eltham, called for refreshment at the house of a miller there. The miller was out; but his pretty young wife was at home, and when the king saw how charming she was he made love to her. Their illicit amour was interrupted by the miller, who returned at an inconvenient moment, and seeing his wife in another man's arms drew his knife and rushed forward intending to kill them both. But when he recognized the man who had wronged him as the king, he halted, stunned for a moment, then put away his weapon and fell on his knees begging for mercy. At the same time, however, he retained enough courage to crave amends. The king, well pleased with the favours he had enjoyed, admitted the justice of the claim and led the miller to the door. There he asked him to name the farthest point of land he could see. It was, said the miller, a point on the Thames near Redriff, as Rotherhithe was then called, which would be a distance of three miles. The king, with a sweep of his arm, then granted the miller all the land between his own small house and that point; but on two conditions: one that he should forgive his wife, the other that he should make an annual pilgrimage to the point every 18th October, the anniversary of the incident, wearing on his head a pair of buck's horns, which he must set up on a pole at the extremity of his land. In addition, an annual fair was granted to the miller on the same date. And to commemorate the grants, according to the legend, the riverside boundary of the miller's property was called Cuckold's Point, and the fair, Horn Fair.

The story has not a particle of truth in it, and in any case is topographically absurd, to say nothing of the historical fact that Cuckold's Point at Rotherhithe was never in the same manor as Charlton. But the Point and the fair were real enough. Mr. Harold Adshead, in an article on Cuckold's Point in *Thames and Medway*, June, 1952, quotes an entry in an Elizabethan diary: "The same day [25th May, 1562] was sett up at the Cuckold Haven, a great May-polle by bochers and fysher-men full of hornes." And Paul Hentzner, the German lawyer who wrote an account of his visit to England in 1598 tells us that at Cuckold's Point there was a pole with horns to which passers by were accustomed to pay homage. We find also that when the Commissioners of Sewers gave orders for the Thames wall to be repaired along this stretch of the river they referred to the length between Miller's Marsh and the mill at Cuckold's Haven at Rotherhithe. Evidently the original pole disappeared at the beginning of the seventeenth century because John Taylor the Water Poet both lamented at its passing and rejoiced at its restoration.

But what of the fair? It was certainly held on the 18th October and the horn was its symbol. Everything that could possibly be made of horn was offered for sale there. Every booth displayed horns on its sign, and horns were worn by most of the merry crowd who frequented it. Gross writes of an unruly mob who used to assemble at Cuckold's Point and go in procession to Charlton Fair wearing horns. So ribald was the crowd in which the men would often be dressed in women's clothes, that Defoe refers to Charlton as "a village famous or rather infamous for that yearly-collected rabble of mad people at Horn Fair."

Such was Horn Fair towards the end of its time; but if we look into its history we find a more credible origin for the fair itself, and a much more honourable explanation of the horns. Shortly after the Conquest the manor of Charlton belonged to the priory of St. Saviour's, Bermondsey, and in 1268 Henry III granted to the prior a weekly market and an annual three-day fair. The reason for the horns being displayed so widely is surely that the date of the fair, 18th

October, is St. Luke's Day, and St. Luke, who is the patron saint of the parish church, has an ox for his symbol. Moreover, it is particularly appropriate that the horns should have been adopted by the fair because St. Luke is said to have been given the ox to emphasize that his gospel brings out the priesthood of Our Lord, and the sacrificial element in the tradition of fairs has already been stressed more than once. The association with the church is further brought out in the endowed sermon preached that day at the parish church.

The fortunes of the fair were not unbroken. No doubt in common with so many others it fell on evil days during the Commonwealth, but it seems to have been almost suspended still earlier—perhaps at the Dissolution. At all events Nicholas Breton, in his *Antidote for the Headache*, published in 1612, says of the custom of wearing horns at Charlton:

> Long time this solemne custome was observed,
>   And Kentish men with others met to feast;
> But latter times are from old fashions swerved,
>   And grown repugnant to this good behest;
> For now ungrateful men these meetings scorn,
> And thanklesse prove to Fortune and the horn,
> For onely now is kept a poor goose fair,
> Where none but meaner people do repair.

But if the fortunes of Horn Fair declined for a time they were to revive—no doubt at the Restoration—and as late as 1770 it was the custom for a procession figuring a king, a queen— somewhat redundantly—a miller with his pretty wife, with attendants, to start out from an inn at Bishopsgate bound for Charlton Fair, followed by a merry crowd, all of whom

> In comely sorts their foreheads did adorne,
> With goodly coronets of hardy horne.

Another of these spurious fairs sprang up at Deptford as a development of the amusements provided to amuse the crowds that came out of London to see the master and brethren of Trinity House paying their annual visit to Trinity House at Deptford. By 1825 this new fair had become so popular that it was worth the great Richardson's while to attend it.

All such fairs had much in common, and only their peculiarities are worth noting—such features, that is to say, as the circuses at Greenwich, and the horns at Charlton. Most fairs asserted their individuality with something of the kind. According to R. H. Horne, Edmonton Fair, for example, was remarkable for offering for sale nothing of any utilitarian value whatever! At Croydon Fair, which opened at midnight, and also at Mitcham, there was the ceremony of the key, which was carried along the principal streets to open the fair. Not until it had passed were the stallholders at liberty to sell.

North of the Thames there was Fairlop Fair in Hainault Forest, which developed out of the annual visits to a small estate he owned there of a certain Daniel Day, a mast- and block-maker of Wapping. For many years before his death in 1767 Day used to collect his rents on the first Monday in July, travelling to Hainault with thirty or forty of his Wapping cronies, most of them mast- and block-makers like himself, in two or three fully rigged ships mounted on carriage frames and drawn by six horses, with Day and his friends seated on "deck" under an awning, like exhibits in a carnival procession. Their destination was the great oak in Hainault Forest, where, in the shade of its huge branches, a feast of beans and bacon was laid for landlord, tenants, and friends. Originally this was a private affair; but so convivial did it become that thousands came out to share the fun and a fair emerged, with pedlars, hucksters, and all the "fun of the fair."

When one of the branches of the Fairlop Oak was torn off in a gale, Day took it to be an omen of his approaching end and had a coffin made from the timber. The tree itself, which had been set on fire accidentally by gipsies encamped under it in 1805, was blown down in the gale of Feburary, 1820. But the Fairlop procession did not cease either with the death of the renowned Daniel or with the destruction of the oak. It was officially abolished by an order of the Commissioners of Woods and Forests in 1853, but in fact survived, at least in token form, to the eighteen-nineties, and even then something of the Fairlop spirit was continued in the annual cyclists' meet at Woodford, which was a rally of cycling clubs, all in fancy dress, who chose Woodford as their assembling point, and from there toured the neighbourhood, collecting money for hospitals. The "Meet," like the fair, was at Midsummer, and nautical costumes were always in favour. There would, in fact, be a ship on occasion, with the cyclists riding inside it. The Woodford Meet seems to have been abandoned during the First World War.

The nearest equivalents to these suburban jollifications to-day are the fairs at Mitcham, Pinner, and Hampstead Heath, all of which are pleasure fairs similar in character to Midsummer Fair at Cambridge, or St. Giles's Fair at Oxford, but with the difference that they have pearly kings and queens in attendance. Pinner's, however, is a genuine fair, held under an Edward III charter on the Wednesday after Whitsuntide, when all the paraphernalia of the fair is disgorged into the streets of the town from Hampstead Heath, whereas Mitcham's, in spite of a claim that it has a charter granted by Elizabeth I in 1598, is a spurious—or to put it more politely, a customary—fair, of which the earliest record so far traced is as late as 1732. It was then held in connection with a horse and cattle fair on waste land in the manor of Biggin and Tamworth. This manor was sold to Messrs. Beaumont & Son, solicitors, of Coggeshall in Essex, gentlemen knowledgeable in antiquarian matters, who turned their knowledge to good account by letting the right to hold a fair on the manorial waste at Mitcham for a rent of £25 per annum. Subsequently they sold their fair rights as lords of the manor to four trustees, who conveyed them to the conservators of Mitcham Common. Several attempts were made to suppress the fair under the provisions of both the Fair Act of 1871 and the Local Government Act of 1894, but nothing was achieved until 1923, when by the terms of the Mitcham Urban District Council Act the fair rights were transferred to the council on payment to the conservators of £294 14s. 6d. compensation, upon which this despised and unwanted fair acquired respectability, and after being an insufferable nuisance for a generation or more it is now opened each 12th August with the most moving demonstrations of civic regard. This year (1952) the mayor and mayoress, attended by the vice-president of the showmen's guild, drove to the fairground in state, and after complimentary speeches and the presentation of bouquets to the ladies, his worship opened the fair by raising and holding aloft a huge gilded key, while a nearby roundabout organ played the National Anthem. Thus far have we travelled from the ribaldries of Charlton and the orgies of Greenwich!

There is one other thing to be mentioned in connection with Mitcham. All along the pavements may be seen at fair time what are called grottoes, similar in design to those used for the Derbyshire well-dressings. A pattern is chalked on the pavement, then filled in with flowers and coloured stones till it looks like a rug.

These, I am told, are sometimes lit up at night by candles, and children stand by them asking for pennies. This delightful custom died out at the beginning of the 1914–18 war, but has recently been revived. In the old days the children used to sing:

> Please remember the grotto; it's only once a year;
> Please give me a ha'penny to spend at Mitcham Fair.
> Father's gone to sea; Mother's gone to fetch him back,
> So please remember me.
>
> My hands are so dirty, my face is so clean,
> I've got a little pocket to put a penny in.
> A ha'penny won't hurt you, a penny won't kill you.
> Tuppence won't put you in the workhouse.
> My, My, happy day. Give me a ha'penny and I'll run away.

In other parts of the country, with the notable exceptions of parts of Devon and Cornwall, such robust jollifications as those at Fairlop and Greenwich were to be found only at the annual hiring fairs—in some places called statute fairs, in others "mops"—which are also spurious, although they have, in fact, legal warrant, though not as fairs, in that they take their name from the various statutes of labourers by which they were regulated. The first of these was enacted to meet the shortage of agricultural labourers in Edward III's reign, and required every able-bodied man to offer himself for service at stated wages. By far the most important statute regulating labour, however, and consequently regulating hiring fairs, was the 1563 Statute of Apprentices, which repealed all previous acts and provided "for the high constables in every shire to hold and continue petty sessions, otherwise called statute sessions," for this purpose. After that, every

110

# Mops

master and mistress, manservant and maidservant came to town at the appointed day—usually at Martinmas[1] or on Old Michaelmas Day—to hear the rates of pay and conditions of service proclaimed for the ensuing year. The scene, though based, perhaps, on an Irish fair, is vividly sketched for us by Isaac Bickerstaffe in his *Love in a Village*:

HODGE. This way, your worship, this way. Why don't you stand aside there? Here's his worship a-coming.
COUNTRYMAN. His worship!
JUSTICE WOODCOCK. Fy! Fy! what a crowd's this! Odds, I'll put some of them in the stocks (striking a fellow). Stand out of the way sirrah.
HODGE. Now, your honour, now the sport will come. The gut-scrapers are here, and some among them are going to sing and dance. Why, there's not the like of our Statute, mun, in five counties; others are but fools to it.
SERVANT MAN. Come, good people, make a ring; and stand out, fellow-servants, as many of you as are willing and able to bear a bob. We'll let my masters and mistresses see we can do something at least; if they won't hire us it shan't be our fault. Strike up the *Servants' Medley*.

Although according to the letter of the law the hiring was for one calendar year from the date of engagement, certain irregularities appear to have been winked at. In some parishes it was the custom to hire servants for fifty-one weeks only in order to prevent settlement rights.[2] Disputes arising out of the various irregularities in hiring agreements were frequently dealt with at Quarter Sessions. And apart from what may be called evasive agreements, there were the inevitable difficulties for those who failed to find employment, or were dissatisfied with their new places when they saw them, to say nothing of unsatisfactory servants. Consequently, what were called "Runaway Mops" were held in some parts of the country. There was one at Henley-in-Arden on the 29th October, and similar hirings at Southam in Warwickshire on three successive Mondays after Old Michaelmas Day.

In offering themselves for employment it was the custom for both men and women to line up according to their calling,

[1] St. Martin's Day is for this reason called Pack-rag day in some places.
[2] See *The Antiquary*, vol. 49 (1913), p. 412.

wearing appropriate emblems. The shepherd would have a lock of wool in his hat, the groom a bit of sponge, the waggoner a few inches of whipcord, the milkmaid a tuft of cowhair, and so on. An Ascension Day fair at Wem in Shropshire was called Rig Fair, or White Apron Fair, because so many young women were to be found there in white aprons, waiting to be hired. Others would be recognized by their distinctive dress, and perhaps older hands would disdain emblems and appear exactly as they worked, the shepherd with his crook, the waggoner with his whip. The young preferred emblems because they could afterwards be discarded, or displaced by something more decorative. Thus as soon as the milkmaid had found a new mistress she substituted a piece of ribbon for the tuft of cowhair, and was then ready to go off with her swain to the pleasure fair. How old this method of hiring is it would be impossible to say. Do we not read in St. Matthew's Gospel that "he went out about the third hour and saw others standing idle in the market place"? Even in London in the Middle Ages it was the custom for labourers to stand with the tools of their trade in Cheapside and at Charing Cross in the early morning, waiting to be hired.

The bond between master and man was sealed by the payment of earnest money, called in some places the hiring-penny, in others the God's penny, because it had been the custom before the Reformation for this to be given to the Church or spent in buying candles for the altar of a favourite saint as a thank-offering. This sum, which might be a shilling about the beginning of the nineteenth century, was spent at booths, and all too often, no doubt, the bumpkin would be tricked out of his shilling if he did not spend it quickly on gingerbread or a fairing for his sweetheart. As the mop was the one day of the year when the entire neighbourhood came together with money in their pockets, its mirth, and not seldom its licentiousness, would be unrestrained.

# CHAPTER VII

# Provincial Fairs and Markets

## I  NORTH

IN the north of England fairs have changed little through
the centuries. The grip of the northern lords—Nevilles,
Percies, Scropes, and Mowbrays—was not easily loosened.
Even the Church, which in most parts of the country superseded such families, gained little, notwithstanding the great
flocks of the abbeys and priories which grazed over thousands
of acres on the moors and fells. The two lines of clerics who
did own fairs on a comparable scale, the archbishops of York
and the bishops of Durham, were themselves princes of the
Church, living in feudal splendour and jealously guarding
their rights. Others might have itching palms; but they could
wrest nothing from a Neville, a Percy, an archbishop of York,
or a bishop with palatine powers such as the bishop of Durham
had. They might get one or two local fairs—such as the one
at Appletreewick, which was granted to the romantic priory
at Bolton in Craven, renowned for its association with the

shepherd Lord Clifford whose story is told by Wordsworth in
*The White Doe of Rystone;* or those of the abbot of Jervaulx,
who had two annual fairs and a weekly market. The one
abbot who did gain valuable fair rights for himself was the
abbot of Meaux, who at the close of the thirteenth century
petitioned the king, praying that he and his successors might
have a market each week at "Wyke, near Mitton-upon-the-
Hulle," and a fair each year on the vigil, feast, and morrow of
the Holy Trinity and the twelve days following. After receiving his charter the abbot assumed complete control of
the town.

It was the horse fairs that mattered most in⁕the north
throughout the Middle Ages, although many of them were
associated with sheep and cattle fairs held on other days. In
1200 King John granted two fairs at Northallerton to Philip
de Poitou, Bishop of Durham, of which the one at Candlemas
was a horse fair—lasting at one time for as long as a month—
attended by dealers from the Continent as well as from every
part of England, while the other, held at the feast of St.
Bartholomew, was referred to by Camden as "the greatest
fair of kine and oxen, and of most resort, that ever I saw in
all my life." It remained one of the "throngest," as they say
in the north, until the nineteenth century; but in 1841 it
succumbed to the greater attractions of Bedale. Later two
other fairs were granted at Northallerton to the bishops of
Durham: St. George's Fair, granted by Queen Mary, and St.
Matthew's, granted by James I.

It would be hard to say which of the many horse fairs of
Yorkshire was the most important. No doubt one succeeded
another in popularity. Besides his fairs at Northallerton the
bishop of Durham had a horse fair at Howden, which in the
later Middle Ages was one of the largest in Europe and attended regularly by the accredited representatives of many
foreign princes and potentates.

There was a pertinent reason for so many northern fairs
being granted to powerful nobles rather than to the Church,
and equally for their being horse fairs. The Norman and
Plantagenet kings had been less inclined to reduce the power
of the northern lords than that of their counterparts in the
southern counties because with the northern lords rested the

responsibility of protecting the marches from the marauding Scots, and to do this they needed both horses and money. There was thus political significance in these horse fairs of the north. It is true that the Percies and Nevilles could become too mighty for the convenience of the central government—that their private armies could become a threat to the south as well as a warning to the north. When this happened, or appeared to have happened, buyers were sent from London to the North Country fairs to make large-scale purchases as a kind of blood-letting.

Similarly many of the markets granted to towns along the Scottish Border were for the adequate victualling of the important castles there. It is for this reason that most of the Border towns are in England, and the traditional custom of laying in stores at the annual, or bi-annual, fair is still maintained, as a visit to Carlisle, or "Carel," fair will prove. Cattle, on the other hand, are now sold at the auction mart. Before this was established 60,000–80,000 head would be sold annually at the autumn fair. In 1887 only 50 were sold.

The conservatism of the pre-industrial north was again turned to account in the seventeenth century, when James II granted charters to several populous towns in the hope of winning the Catholic north to his side, and thus reducing the fear of rebellion. The burgesses of Doncaster were granted livestock fairs on every alternate Saturday from Easter to the feast of St. Andrew the Apostle by Charles II. Then in 1685 James II, for political reasons, granted them two three-day fairs, one from the 15th November, the other from the Monday next before the feast of the Purification.

The most amazing thing about the traditional and conspicuously unsuccessful attempt to keep out the Scots is that it should have been kept up, in show if not in earnest, long after the Union of the Crowns. At Alnwick in Northumberland, for example, there are records that watch and ward was kept until 1737, although towards the end it appears to have been maintained only fitfully. The custom was for the bailiff of the manor to lead the local officials and the more substantial tenants to the castle on the first day of the fair, and after seeing that they were adequately regaled with wine, to return with them in procession to the market cross, where the fair was proclaimed. When that had been done, all the townships owing suit and service to the barony were called upon to provide watch and ward. Those selected for the duty were armed with ancient and totally inadequate weapons, and, after taking an oath, were stationed at the entrances to the town for the express purpose of keeping out the Scots, who after the union of the two countries, were, of course, allowed to enter without hindrance, and were probably welcomed. The reason for this farcical custom being maintained was that the service freed the townships concerned from market tolls for a twelvemonth.

There were other mock survivals of the old Border feuds, and the memory of the fights themselves was kept alive at Alnwick by the children, who used to muster in front of the castle gates with immense supplies of pine cones for use as ammunition, and well and truly did they pelt each other! The natural fighting spirit of the northern character usually found expression sooner or later at these fairs. At best it found an outlet in vigorous games or contests of skill between rival communities, at worst it broke out in drunken brawls in market squares or alehouse yards towards midnight. In the Percy country particularly, the lord of the manor charged his officers to maintain order on these occasions, and sometimes the force used was pretty drastic. Thus in Henry Best's *Farming Book* (1641) we read that "at the last Driffield Whitsuntide fayer the men of Nafferton and Lowthorpe came with clubbes, to keep good order and rule the faire, and have a piper to playe before them."

The duke's pipers were in attendance at most of these Northumberland fair proclamations. At the fair at Bewick's birthplace, Avingham, for instance, the proclamation procession, which was called "riding the fair," was led from the principal inn by two of the duke's pipers dressed in the pale blue Percy livery with white capes, wearing the cognizance of a silver half-moon, followed by the bailiff and tenantry. The ceremony, vividly described in Hone's *Every-day Book*, was no doubt typical of all the larger fairs in the Percy country. And this ceremonial procession of the duke's representatives had its popular counterpart on what was called "Gwonny Jokesane's Day," when a mock "mayor" was

elected, and he and his supporters went in procession round
the village, first calling on the minister, whom the "mayor,"
after the company had entertained his reverence with a dance,
addressed in such terms as: "A yez! twa times A yez! an'
three times A yez! If ony man or ony man's man, laird, loons,
lubberdoons, dogs, skelpers, gabbrigate swingers, shall com-
mit a parliament as a twarliment, we, in the township o'
Avingham, shall hea his legs, and heid, tied ta th' cagwheel,
an' gwonny Jokesane's day." The minister then shook hands
with the "mayor" and treated the company to his home-
brewed ale. The ceremony was repeated at every large house
in the village, and at each there was a similar reception.

Nor were the Percies the only feudal family to maintain
such customs until the end of the nineteenth century. A
similar one survived at Dalton-in-Furness until the eighteen-
nineties. There every 24th October a number of javelin men
attended the Duke of Buccleuch's steward for the ancient
proclamation ceremony, in which the duke was referred to as
"lord of the late dissolved monastry and manor of Furness,"
and it was ordered that "no person or persons have or bear
any habiliments of war, steel coats, bills or battle axes, but
such as are appointed to attend upon the said steward during
this present fair." This at least as late as 1891!

The value of the horse, however, was not dependent upon
the provocation of the Scot, and horse fairs have continued
to be of prime importance in the northern counties. So great
indeed has been the Yorkshireman's pride in the horse that
for centuries a traveller had only to whistle at the gates of
the principal hostelry of any town in England for a brisk, if
sometimes ill-mannered, Yorkshire groom to present himself.
Nothing would keep a North Country sportsman away from
a horse fair. It is told of John Peel that he was going to a
horse fair on the day his wife gave birth to twins. One child
was delivered and John was told that another was on the
way. He replied with spirit that he didn't care if there were
four, he was going to the fair.

One of the oldest of the Yorkshire horse fairs, that at Lee
Gap, has been held continuously for nearly 800 years without
a break, and although it is no longer an international mart,
it is still the most popular horse fair in the East Riding. Mr.

J. Fairfax-Blakeborough, in the *Yorkshire: East Riding*
volume of the "County Books" series, in referring to these
Yorkshire horse fairs, quotes an article on Howden Fair
in the *Sporting Magazine* for 1807, in which it was estimated
that no fewer than 2,000 horses would be in and around
Howden each night while the fair lasted, and as many more
would be put up in the stables and fields of every village
within 10 miles. These would all be sold next day—that is
to say: at the beginning of the nineteenth century approximately 4,000 horses would be sold daily. And as late as 1874
the *Yorkshire Post* reported that Howden Fair still held its
own.

Historically, the two most interesting North Country fairs
are those at Brough Hill and Stagshaw Bank, both of which
were almost certainly of Roman origin. It was of Brough Hill
Fair, held annually by right of a charter granted by Edward
III to Robert de Clifford in 1330, that Gray, in his *Journal of
a Tour*, wrote on the 30th September, 1769: "A mile and a
half from Brough on a hill lay a great army encamped. It was
the Brough cattle fair. On nearer approach appeared myriads
of horses and cattle on the road itself; and in all the fields
round me a brisk stream hurrying across the way; thousands
of clean, healthy people, in their best parti-coloured apparel,
farmers and their families, esquires and their daughters,
hastening up from the hills and down the fell on every
side, glittering in the sun, and pressing forward to join the
throng."

The very mention of Brough Hill Fair is enough to raise
the spirits of any Yorkshireman worth his salt. Its continued
prosperity was due to its being held at the time of year when
stock was being sold off the fells. It was the great North
Riding fair for the sale of unbroken fell and dale ponies, and
was attended not only by farmers and dealers, but also by
Durham mine owners, who bought their pit ponies at Brough,
and tradesmen from the industrial areas of the West Riding
who needed van ponies. Above all, Brough Hill Fair was the
great rallying place for North Country gipsies, who seemed
to set the hill ablaze with their gay costumes and garishly
painted caravans. And in fact at the end of the fair they
sometimes did set the hill ablaze, for if there was a moon,

and the night was fine, they would light huge bonfires and dance till dawn.

For days before the fair was held, strings of ponies were to be seen along every road and green track—the old drove roads —from the fells of Yorkshire, Westmorland, and Cumberland, trotting towards Brough, as well as great herds of Scots cattle drifting slowly down from the Highlands. On the lonely tracks now used only by hikers these herds and droves passed year by year through the centuries, and at cottage doors where ice-cream is sold to-day, or where a board is hung out in the summer months to announce that teas are served indoors, stalls would be set up before and after Brough Hill Fair and spread out with the real old country meat and drink —home-brewed ale, or jugs of tea, and enormous game-pies with crust the like of which we haven't seen since we became a Welfare State. Such scenes are only memories now, and Brough Hill Fair, as the old folks will tell you, is not what it was.

Romaldkirk Fair, held on the Thursday after Brough Hill, was founded to sell off the unsold stock from Brough. More important was Appleby June Fair, which originally had days for sheep and cattle, but for the last fifty years or so has been a horse fair only, and like its neighbour, Brough, a great place for gipsy tinkers and horse-copers who, since Gallows Hill was enclosed in 1911, have been forced to encamp on the wide grass verges of the roads. Sometimes there will be as many as 1,000 caravans lining the roads for nearly 2 miles, the old folks sitting on stools and chairs by the roadside till midnight, quietly smoking their stubby clay pipes; the young, as at Brough, dancing in the roadway till dawn. There is nothing to match these scenes anywhere else in England.

The other North Country fair mentioned a moment ago, that at Stagshaw Bank, was the great sheep fair, at which upwards of 100,000 head would be sold at the end of the eighteenth century, when Stagshaw Bank was in its prime. A valuable description of the scene is to be found in Dr. Raine's memoir of his friend the Rev. John Hodgson, author of the *History of Northumberland.*[1] Its situation near Corbridge and the Roman Wall, some distance away from any great centre

[1] See *Notes and Queries*, 5th Series, viii, p. 269.

of population at the time it flourished, makes it reasonably certain that Stagshaw Bank Fair was established to meet the needs of the large population brought into a sparsely populated region to build the Wall. For detailed information about Stagshaw Bank, as about Brough, we must turn to the Durham records, which from the thirteenth century onwards have references to both these ancient fairs, chartered by early sovereigns for the sake of their revenues.

Another Northumberland fair, the "Whitsun-Tryste" held on a hill near Wooler, is mentioned in Lockhart's *Life of Scott.*

Most of the North Country cattle and sheep fairs have either dwindled to insignificance or disappeared entirely, notwithstanding their charters. Stagshaw Bank Fair was held for the last time on the 22nd May and the 5th July, 1926. It was abolished under the Fairs Act of 1871 by a Home Office Order dated 5th March, 1927. But although sheep and cattle fairs count for less now than they did at one time, and were never as famous as the great horse fairs, it must not be thought that the north was unmindful of the economic importance of sheep. The warrior tradition did eventually give place to the industrial over the greater part of the region, and Yorkshire, as all the world knows, gained pre-eminence in the wool trade. The one great civilizing force of the Middle Ages, the Church, did not lose all knowledge of these northern counties which played so vital a part in the original conversion of England to Christianity. Beverley's three fairs, at one time marts of international importance, were unique in Yorkshire in having the declared support of Pope Adrian IV, who issued a bull to secure the peace at them. The abbeys did prosper, even if few of them owned fairs, and wool was the foundation of their wealth then as it has been the foundation of Yorkshire's wealth ever since. If the Yorkshireman's heart is with his horses, his head has always been ready enough to tot up his sheep, and sheep are still the principal topic of conversation in all the inns of the North Riding—between races anyhow—where practically every caller has a sheep-dog at his heels. Sheep-dog trials are still the most popular sport, even at pleasure fairs. And one Yorkshire town, Skipton, takes its name from the animal which, however weak its head may be, can be said to have carried the nation on its back for centuries. Skipton, that is to say, is sheep-town, and a local record shows that the former lords of Skipton, the earls of Albemarle, had Saturday markets granted by King John in 1204, and two fairs, one at the feast of St. Martin, the other at the feast of St. James.

After the Dissolution, the wool sales of the Cistercian abbeys gave place to the cloth markets, which produced so many Yorkshire towns along the lines already described in the chapter entitled "Fairs into Markets." The Yorkshire antiquary, Ralph Thoresby, records in his Diary that on the 14th August, 1710, he rode with the mayor of Leeds and others to interview Lord Irwin about the erection of a hall in Kirkgate for the sale of white cloths, in order to prevent the trade of the town being drawn away to Wakefield, always the most determined rival of Leeds, where such a hall had recently been built. The following year Leeds did get its cloth hall, and Thoresby observed with satisfaction that people were summoned to the weekly market by "a bell in a beautiful cupola painted and gilt." Such markets had been developing throughout the north, and particularly in the West Riding, since the middle of the sixteenth century.

October is the month for sheep fairs, and the bleating of the flocks is still to be heard over the fells as one answers another along the old packhorse trails that go higher up the mountains than the drove roads already mentioned. Down these the sheep are driven to reach the road by crossing one of the old packhorse bridges, built with low parapets so that the packs of wool on the ponies' backs could swing clear of them when they were brought down to market from the weavers' cottages on the lonely fellsides. No one has described these Yorkshire sheep-fairs more vividly than Halliwell Sutcliffe, who in *Striding Dales* writes: "Kettlewell Sheep Fair was in progress, a fair in keeping with the grim, limestone crags that shield the narrow meadows and the pastures on either side Wharfe River. It is a gathering not to be missed by any lover of the Dale. The first glimpse of it is the story of bygone days that live on among us. Constant to types inbred by the generations, the thick-set farmers gather, and the wise sheep-dogs, and the ewes bleating with a sorrow that will not be quiet. Above them are the ancient hills that know no changes, save in winter's cold and summer's heat. The men and the bleating ewes, the bright-eyed dogs, seem old as the hills, and as young.

"The colouring of the scene is unforgettable on such a day as this. Grey-green fells, grey walls, russet bracken-slopes above; below, grey sheep and brown coats and gaiters of the buyers and the sellers; grey wood smoke from the clustered chimney-stacks, rising against sober russet of the trees—all in a blended harmony."

On most of the northern moors sheep-rearing had been introduced by Scandinavian shepherd stock, who reached England by way of Ireland. The dales, however, with their fresh sweet grass were settled by Danish stock, who introduced cattle-rearing. Eventually Yorkshire had two distinct breeds of cows, the short-horned Holderness in the east, and the long-horned Craven in the west. Both were bred for milk—increasingly as the growing towns of the West Riding demanded ever greater supplies. Beef cattle had to be brought from Scotland, so in the eighteenth century Scots drovers, with great herds of black cattle, were a familiar sight on the northern roads. Later they were to wander down into East Anglia and even to the Home Counties. Defoe describes them, and there is a delightful story told to this day at Halesworth in Suffolk about a Peter McDougal who sold cattle at Norwich, Ipswich, Bury St. Edmunds and other East Anglian markets. Because he got so much more per head than anyone else could obtain, rumours got round that he was in league with the devil, and as Peter did nothing to discourage the belief his reputation for supernatural cunning increased until one day at Halesworth cattle fair two or three admirers tried to pump him:

"Tell'un yer secret, mun," they pleaded, "You ha' med twelve pun a yead by a lot as aren't woth sex."

They took Peter off to the local pub, "The Case is Altered," and plied him hard with whisky and a supper of hot steak-pudding well savoured with pepper and onions until he was really merry, then gathered round him again and pleaded with him to share with them his secret. Peter, looking more roguish than usual with his plaid thrown over his left shoulder, and his blue bonnet cocked over his right eye, laid down his pipe by his empty glass and in broad Scots said: "I'll tell ye.

# Cattle Dealing

Ye'd knoo hoo I coom to make sae good a price by my
beasties? Weel, I'll tell ye. I ken it's just this, I find a fule
and sell to him."

Some drovers, however, were not so cunning as Peter, and
never did sell their cattle. At the end, wearied with long
travelling, they would turn the unsold beasts loose on a
common or piece of roadside waste and go off to try and get
a job for themselves. But, on the whole, cattle-dealing became
an extremely profitable business in the eighteenth and nineteenth centuries, and Englishmen themselves began to cross
the Border for cattle. The first to import them in great numbers was a Malham man named John Birtwhistle,[1] who was
financed by the British Linen Bank, and as early as 1745
would have as many as 5,000 beasts on his land at a time,
with twice that number on the roads. As soon as they had
recovered from their long journey these would be sold at
privately organized "fairs" on his own vast field of about
730 acres watered by Malham Tarn. Others followed Birtwhistle's example and large fortunes were amassed at one
time by North Country cattle-dealers. Ralph Robb of Top-
cliffe, near Thirsk, one of the Earl of Egremont's tenants, in
the early years of the nineteenth century travelled to Falkirk
Fair with £30,000 in Bank of England notes. He returned
with 12,000 head of cattle, having drawn bills for the balance
of their price.[2]

Fairs for the sale of farm produce other than livestock
have now practically disappeared from the northern counties,
although the name is retained for the monthly cheese sales
at Preston and Lancaster, and the quarterly leather sales at
Leeds. Yarm in the North Riding, which has a three-day
October cheese fair held under a charter granted by King
John, is probably the outstanding exception. As in other
parts of the country, markets have taken the place of fairs,
and since the eighteen-seventies, privately owned auction
marts have largely displaced both for the sale of livestock.
Nevertheless, the northern counties, like the midland and

[1] Thomas Hartley: *Natural Curiosities in the Environs of Malham in
Craven, Yorkshire,* 1786 *and* 1834.
[2] *A Family History: The Wyndhams of Norfolk and Somerset,* vol. ii,
p. 304.

southern, are still thickly strewn with markets. Lancashire alone has 164; the West Riding of Yorkshire has 130. About 80 per cent of these are owned by local authorities and, in the industrial areas, have lost their traditional character. That is to say, local produce is not so prominent as it remains in the pannier markets of the west. For all that, those of us who cherish regional characteristics will always look for the small round cheeses so familiar in the dales at such markets as those of Richmond and Barnard Castle, and for local farm butter in all the markets between Carlisle and Preston.

The Rufford Village Museum has a collection of wooden butter prints, some of which have the traditional heart motif used for the round pounds of butter sent to market from Ormskirk, others the rose motif used on the rectangular pounds from Preston.

In Lancashire one looks also for poultry. The county of the red rose has by far the greatest number of fowls per acre of any in the kingdom, and while fruit and vegetables are not grown in the north as they are in the south, we do find large potato markets. But the needs of such places as Liverpool, Manchester, Leeds, and Bradford have become so great that the northern counties can no longer meet them, and the coming together of townsfolk and country folk on market day has gone for ever from the larger towns. On the other hand, the municipally controlled markets in these great centres of population are far better managed than any in the south. What appears to have been the first market hall consciously designed for modern needs was the one built about 1819 at Liverpool, where all the markets are owned by the corporation. The area of the Stanley site alone, all of which is covered, is 82,280 square yards, apart from the roadways.

The livestock to supply meat for industrial Lancashire and Yorkshire is bought in such auction marts as those of York, Carlisle, and Salford; but store cattle and sheep are still bought in such old-time markets as those of Alston Moor, Bolton Fell, and Roadhead in Cumberland; Bellingham, Haltwhistle and Scotsgap in Northumberland. Keswick has a fair for the disposal of the hardy little Herdwick sheep known to every Lakeland climber, and markets for the rough fell breeds are held at Horton in Westmorland, at Muker,

WOODEN BUTTER-MOULDS

# Lancashire Fish Stones

Reeth, and Masham in Yorkshire. In fact sheep sales are held regularly in most of the dale towns and larger villages.

Crops are grown in quantity only in the east, near the coast, and up the Eden valley to Penrith. Elsewhere the country is divided between the rough little sheep that crop the fells and moors, and the dairy herds found particularly in the Craven country. It is not always appreciated that the industrialized West Riding, which also has vast moors suitable only for rough grazing, still has half its total acreage in rich pasture land.

Of architectural memorials of ancient fairs and markets the north has few. Covered crosses are practically unknown, and few of the old market houses remain. Such as there are, therefore, are all the more noteworthy. The Lake District has several. Perhaps the most characteristic reminder of old-style marketing is the market place at Cartmell, with its pillar cross raised on wide steps for the farmers' wives to set out their baskets of butter and eggs, and its old fish-stones—rough hewn stone tables that in pre-Reformation times were a feature of North Country markets, but are now rare. Poulton-le-Fylde has them. At Lancaster and Kirkham they formed a circle; at Preston, an oval.  But if there are few market crosses that are architecturally important, there are inumerable market places in the Lake District and the Yorkshire dales that retain their old-world character, and where a larger proportion of business is still done by the farmers' wives on market day than in any other part of the country, with the possible exception of the west Midlands. We think of Settle, Leyburn, Bedale, and many others—most notably, perhaps, Ripon, which Defoe thought "the finest and most beautiful square that is to be seen of its kind in England." There are also a few of the old mark stones that in many places became market stones, and upon which, or near which, market crosses were later set up. In Scarborough museum, for example, there is a blue stone said to be the old market stone used for the ratification of sales in the traditional Yorkshire manner: that is to say, with a slap of the buyer's hand on the extended palm of the seller in the manner already described at Middleham. If there are few market bells, except in Lancashire, it is because it was the custom, as I was told at Masham, for the church bells to

129

be rung, so that the sound would travel a greater distance and help to guide travellers crossing the moors to fair or market.

Other reminders of the evolution of the market are to be found in the north in the naming of fairs. In some places they are still called feasts; in others, tides; and in others again, wakes, the name used now for the annual holidays in Lancashire. In the old days bear-baiting was the great attraction at many of these annual celebrations. Wake, of course, has a far-reaching significance, and it is therefore not surprising that in some places ancient yews should mark the site of fairs surviving from wakes. Langsett in Yorkshire comes to mind as an instance, and there the manorial court was held at the same point. Incidentally, there is a similar instance of a fair surviving from a wake, held on Palm Sunday, at Crowhurst in Surrey. At Howley, near Batley, in Yorkshire, where a fair replaced a wake, the site was near an ancient chapel and holy well, and there the name as well as the event fell away from sanctity. Field Cock Fair was formerly Field Kirk Fair.

But if there are fewer architectural memorials than elsewhere, there are ceremonies in plenty. At Scarborough, for instance, it was the custom for the local officials to ride round the town in procession when the fair was to be proclaimed, their hats and horses' heads bedecked with flowers, and at each halting place for the town crier to read a rhymed proclamation, which began:

> Lords, gentlemen, and loons,
> Ye're welcome to our toons
> Until St. Michael's Day,
> But tolls and customs pay
> From Latter Lammas Day.

In true Yorkshire fashion the proclamation concluded with an invitation to "sport and play," but also with a warning that there must be "nowt amiss."

The most interesting of these customs is that of dog-whipping, found at several fairs in the vicinity of York as well as in the city itself, where it originated, according to tradition, because one day a dog, which was evidently lying

130

hidden under the altar table, ran off with the consecrated pax, dropped accidentally by a priest who was celebrating mass, whereupon the enraged clergy of the city ordered that in future all dogs found either on the streets of York or of any town within sixty miles of it, on the anniversary of the profanation, should be pursued and flogged to death.

Such cruelty, and the hue and cry that went with it, is best forgotten. It is not what we think of first when North Country fairs and markets are mentioned. Rather do we see the sturdy figures of dalesman driving their flocks down the ancient tracks, their progress accompanied by shrill whistles as they signal their dogs sent out to round up stragglers, or hear the lowing of cattle, a sound that echoes from crag to crag as the herds drift down to fair or market. Such sights and sounds as these, however, now become rarer as more and more livestock are transported in vans and waggons. But if the traditional sights and sounds of the old fairs become less familiar, the metallic blare of a roundabout organ, which carries 10 miles or more, still summons the young folk from grey stone village and farmstead as effectively as any Percy or Mowbray trumpeter. And if anyone suspects a decline in the traditional fairtime spirit in northern England, let him visit the Michaelmas Crab Fair at Egremont, at which crab apples are thrown out as a reminder of the days when the lord of the manor distributed largesse to his people as he rode the bounds of the fair, although the name, we may think, must originally have referred to the animal rather than the apple.

## II MIDLAND

The Scots were not the only cattle thieves to be feared at English fairs and markets. On the west there were the Welsh, who were almost equally incursive at one time. It was to afford protection against these that the Conqueror created Hugh Lupus, his nephew, Earl of Chester, and gave him full palatine powers within the Roman city and for a radius of 8 miles from its walls. This same Hugh, surnamed Lupus for his ferocity, founded the abbey of St. Werburgh and granted it a three days' fair at the patronal festival, with all the usual rights and privileges. So this first of Chester's

chartered fairs was held in February. But as the second
charter, granted by Earl Randle between 1208 and 1211,
which is now in the city muniment room, refers to Midsummer [1] and Michaelmas fairs, each of fifteen days' duration,
Chester was evidently a great trading centre at an early date,
and its fair or fairs may be assumed to be of great antiquity,
predating by centuries the granting of the charters. It may
have been the early enjoyment of trading privileges that made
the burgesses so fractious under the abbot's rule at fairtime
until a settlement was negotiated between them in the time
of Edward I. If so, the abbot would have been entitled to
remind the burgesses of the protection they enjoyed.

Thrilling stories are told of the audacity of the Welsh in
their raids on Chester Fair. In Earl Randle's time there was
the never-to-be forgotten occasion when Roger de Lacy,
Constable of Chester, rallied to the earl's standard for the
defence of the city a motley rout of fiddlers, stage-players,
cobblers, and mountebanks both male and female, in such
numbers that the Welsh raised the siege and fled. In recom-
pense de Lacy was given exclusive authority over all fiddlers,
shoemakers, minstrels, and the flotsam and jetsam of the
fairtime population. Very prudently he retained for himself
and his heirs authority over the shoemakers, but passed on
the minstrels, players, and so forth to his steward, Dutton of
Dutton. Eventually, however, the Welsh discovered that they
could do better for themselves by offering their friezes, linsey-
wolsey, and blankets for sale at the fair than by risking
broken heads for a few cattle, especially as fairtime was the
only time when strangers were allowed to bring goods into
Chester for sale. But even when trade had again proved itself
the best instrument of peace, the need for defence was not
forgotten. The tolls received at the fairs were called "murage."
They were set aside for keeping the city walls in repair.

To other fairs along the Border, particularly to those of
Shropshire, the Welsh drove in their cattle, eventually pene-
trating to the heart of England and as far south as Barnet,
where Welsh cattle were being sold for the London market
from the fourteenth century. As early as 1312 700 cattle from
north Wales were sent to Windsor for use in the king's house-

[1] St. Werburgh's Translation.

hold. Indeed the court, as well as many castles and abbeys, was being supplied with meat from Wales in the fourteenth century, while in the fifteenth, Welsh cattle were killed and salted for feeding Henry V's army in France—a record is still extant of the salting of ninety-three of them for the troops at Calais.[1] Later, of course, when the Midlands had been industrialized, great droves were driven in from mid and south Wales to be fattened on the grazing land of Leicestershire and Northamptonshire, and from north Wales into Warwickshire, for sale at the great markets of the new and constantly growing towns. Nor was the London market neglected. In the 1880s a Welshman named Harris never failed to bring two or three hundred beasts to the November fair at Hertford, where he hired a private field called Plough Mead to sell them in.

But to return to Chester: the site of the great October fair, which became the more important of the city's two fairs that continued to prosper, was at the junction of the city's two main thoroughfares—in the shadow, that is to say, of St. Peter's church, from the battlements of which hung the famous Chester Hand or Glove, a symbol of the sign manual authorizing the fair, and a guarantee of justice and protection for those who bought and sold in it.[2] Nearby stood the market cross, from which the fair was proclaimed until Cromwell's men destroyed it after the siege, and the narrow streets that converged on this central point were so packed with merchandise that the showmen and minstrels had to be put into the old Justing-field outside the east wall. The costliest fabrics would be displayed, no doubt, on stalls along the protected balconies of the rows until the time came for the wealthier merchants to hire rooms in the inns, and finally to build halls similar to the Yorkshire Cloth Halls in which Ralph Thoresby was so interested. The Manchester merchants had one of their own. There was also a Union Hall for general trade, and a Linen Hall. Fairs were thus of great importance at Chester and figure prominently in histories of the town.

[1] Skeel, "Cattle Trade between England and Wales from the 15th to the 19th centuries," *Royal Hist. Soc. Trans.*, 1926, 4th Series, lx, pp. 136–8.
[2] See article by R. Stewart-Brown, "The Chester Hand or Glove." *Chester Arch. Soc. Journal*, vol. xx, p. 124.

The fragments of Chester's market cross, which had been buried near St. Peter's church, were subsequently dug up and, about 1900, were set up as an ornament in the grounds of Netherleigh House.

The Midlands in general have remained rich in crosses and market houses, particularly in the stone regions of the west where local gilds flourished. Many, notwithstanding what they suffered from excesses of Puritan zeal in Cromwell's time, are still of great beauty. At Abingdon, where the present fine building is at least the fourth on the site, Leland found "a fine house with open pillars coverid with a rofe of leade for market fokes," which he describes as "a right goodly crosse of stone with fair degres and imagerie." And so, apparently, the people of Coventry thought, because a copy of a contract for building a cross there, after the model of the one at Abingdon, at a cost of £197 6s. 8d., is preserved in the British Museum.[1] This particular cross at Abingdon was replaced by another before 1569, after having stood since the earlier cross—which itself may not have been the first—was burnt down in the riots of 1327. The present building dates from between 1672 and 1682 and replaces the third cross, which was destroyed by Waller's men in 1644. Most of its stone—certainly the ornamental parts—came from the quarries at Burford.

Of Abingdon's October Fair, *Jackson's Oxford Journal* reported that in 1805, when there were upwards of 10,000 people present, there was a "great show of dairy maids, who were hired at very low wages, owing to the late reduced price of cheese. The taskers went off briskly, and at high prices, the Farmers being in a hurry to get their corn thrashed out for market. The numerous gang of pickpockets who attended began to exercise their dexterity very early in the day; and (while the attention of the populace was excited by the beauty of the Grand Turk's Palace, the wonderful feats of The Little Strong woman, and the harmony of the Pentonville Organ) contrived to empty the pockets of a poor woman of about forty shillings, a countryman of about £3 and a farmer of his pocket book, containing notes to a considerable amount." The report continues with a lengthy dissertation on the attractions of a menagerie of wild beasts, and feats of a nimble

[1] Add. MS. 666, p. 432.

134

African, i.e. a monkey, Adam's Royal Troop of Equestrians and German Musicians, and of the Learned Little Horse. "In the evening a number of fine young men were enlisted by the recruiting parties for his Majesty's service." Twenty-nine years later we find the same journal reporting that the June pleasure fair, "once so noted in the Ock-street for country cousins, hams, and gooseberry pie, approached somewhat its former eclat; though prostitutes, pickpockets, highwaymen, footpads, and swindlers made a much larger display than usual."

A less familiar cross than Abingdon's is that at Rothwell in Northamptonshire, presented to the town about 1577 by Sir Thomas Tresham, a neighbouring squire whose loyalty to the old church, for which several of his family suffered, led to many of his beneficent schemes being abandoned when he was cast into prison for harbouring the Jesuit martyr, Edmund Campion.

Rothwell is in hunting country, midway between Pytchley and Market Harborough, and had a famous horse fair looked forward to with special interest by the Blue Coat Pensioners of Jesus Hospital, because on Fair Sunday they were always supplied with new coats and breeches. It was also the custom thereabouts to get all the kitchens, cellars, and outhouses limewashed by fair day. Horse fairs were common in this part of the region, while, in other parts of the Midlands, Biggleswade had a famous one, Bampton in Oxfordshire one held on the 26th August, which was granted to William de Vallence by Henry III, and Defoe tells us how surprised he was in Staffordshire to find so flourishing a fair as the one at Penkridge, 6 miles south of Stafford. "We expected nothing extraordinary," he says, "but was I say surpriz'd to see the prodigious number of horses brought hither, and those not ordinary and common draught-horses, and such kinds as we generally see at country-fairs remote from London. But here were really incredible numbers of the finest and most beautiful horses that can anywhere be seen; being brought hither from Yorkshire, the bishoprick of Durham, and all the horse-breeding countries. We were told that there were not less than an hundred jockies and horse-kopers, as they call them there, from London, to buy horses for sale. Also an incredible number of gentlemen attended with their grooms to buy gallopers, or race-horses, for their Newmarket sport. In a word, I believe I may mark it for the greatest horse-fair in the world, for horses of value, and especially those we call saddle-horses. There are indeed greater fairs for coach-horses, and draught horses; though here were great numbers of fine large stone horses for coaches, &c., too. But for saddle-horses, for the light saddle, hunters, pads, and racers, I believe the world cannot match this fair.''

The point to keep constantly in mind in considering Midland fairs—and it is indicated in the above quotation from Defoe—is that they have stood in the same topographical and economic relationship to the country as a whole as the market square has to the town. Consequently they have been, as it were, clearing centres for the rest of the country. Thus most of the horses sold at Midland fairs were brought in from other parts—Irish and Welsh ponies and horses as well as Yorkshire and Durham breeds. It was the same with produce. It is from Defoe again that we learn that cheeses were bought by factors at the great cheese fair at Atherstone for resale to the people of East Anglia at Sturbridge. Similarly, the fair and market at Royston on the old North Road, granted by Richard I, was formerly so much frequented by corn merchants and maltsters from neighbouring counties that many of the old accounts of this part of the country refer to teams of horses laden with corn as a familiar sight on the roads for miles around. Again, Morton, in the *Natural History of Northampton-shire*, describes his county as being ''in the trade way,'' and says that one of the Towcester inns (in 1712) was reputed to have the best custom of any inn on the Chester road.

But over most of the region the wealth of the countryside was in its livestock, particularly in its cattle, which is what we should expect with such dairy-farming counties as Cheshire and Shropshire, and in the old days Staffordshire. These, of course, supplied both fairs and markets with a rich assortment of cheeses, and, when the region became industrialized, with milk. The Midlands abound in livestock markets. We think, to name a few, of those at Shrewsbury, Gloucester, Hereford, Oswestry, Rugby, Northampton, Leicester, and Derby. And each has a long history. Counties that are now largely industrialized still maintain a vigorous rural economy—as well they may in view of their long-established traditions. Stafford-shire, mentioned a moment ago, was particularly famous for its grazings in Camden's day, when, by the way, cattle were immediately thought of as producing leather as well as milk, beef, and cheeses. Indeed, when the old chroniclers in their folios attempted to sum up the goods offered for sale at fairs, hides and skins were always included:

> Hides and fish, salmon, hake, herringe,
> Irish wool and linen cloth, faldinge,
> And martens good, be her marchandie,
> Hartes hides, and other of venerie,
> Skins of otter, squirrel, and Irish hare,
> Of sheep, lamb and foxe, is her chaffare,
> Fells of kids and conies in great plenty.

Spring and autumn cattle fairs, then, were general through-out the Midlands until markets and auction marts replaced them. And some that are situated in what we are now inclined to think of as recently established industrial towns, such as Luton, are in fact of great antiquity.

Apart from the Cotswolds and Shropshire, sheep fairs are less common, although Leicester and Nottingham have them, and there are sheep fairs at Bicester, and at Market Ilsley on the Oxford to Southampton road. The animal of exceptional importance in the Midlands is the pig. Even to-day there is more pork and its products sold in Birmingham than any-where else in the kingdom. And apart from the economic aspect, there is something particularly appropriate in the thought of herds of pigs, or swine, as they were called, roam-ing through the stubble fields and racing across the heaths of these Midland shires: foraging for beech mast and acorns in the great forests of Sherwood or Shakespeare's Arden, because the pig goes back in the English scene as far as history can trace and farther. Mortimer, in his *Whole Art of Husbandry* (1707), remarks that the fattest were to be found in Northamptonshire and Leicester, in the latter of which—in bean-bellied Leicester—their diet was greatly enriched with peas and beans. Unfortunately, pig fairs are extremely rare, and probably no fair was ever chartered solely, or was mainly, for the sale of pigs. The reasons for this lack, no doubt, are the obvious ones. In the old days every cottager kept and killed his own pig, and, still more to the point, the pig could not be driven long distances, as horses and cattle could when shod, so had to be sold at the weekly markets, whither it goes in nursery rhyme and country lore time out of mind.

A detailed study of the scores of important fairs and markets of the Midlands—as of every other region—is beyond the scope of this general summary; but in view of the peculiar characteristics already enumerated it is easy to understand the fame of such places as Northampton, Nottingham, Leicester, and other Midland towns. Northampton, in fact, was granted one fair after another until in 1849 there were no fewer than thirteen of them. Subsequently the wool fair was dropped, but there were still twelve fairs listed in the 1931 Kelly's Directory. Most of them, curiously enough, are comparatively modern. There were only two in 1566: St. George's and St. Hugh's. But the charter of 1599 refers to, and sanctions, seven, and the number was increased as need arose right down to the nineteenth century. For all that, the golden age for Northampton so far as its fairs are concerned was the mediæval, when cloth was bought there, as at St. Ives, for the royal household. In 1231, for example, William de Haverhill and William the king's tailor had orders to buy at Northampton Fair 150 robes for the knights of the royal household, 100 robes for clerks and sergeants, 5 for grooms, and 300 tunics for alms.[1] Few English fairs can have exceeded it in importance in the thirteenth century, at the beginning of which it was held in All Saints church and churchyard. In 1325, however, Henry III ordered that future fairs should be in "a void and waste place to the north of the church." From this, along the lines already traced as general, the great market square developed. It was this order incidentally, that prompted Bishop Grosseteste to prohibit the holding of fairs in sacred places throughout his diocese.

The fair we may think of as the greatest fair of the Midlands to-day, Nottingham Goose Fair, also produced a noble square. The commercial side of this renowned event has gone; but a three-day pleasure fair is still held on the first Thursday

[1] Cal. *Close Rolls*, 1231–4, p. 1, quoted Muncey.

138

in October and the two following days. Alas! no ceremony attends the occasion. Since 1874 even Nottingham Goose Fair has been opened by a printed notice instead of by the traditional proclamation.

The name of this Nottingham fair may puzzle us in this secular age. Clearly it was derived from the holding of the fair at Michaelmas,

> when by Custom (right divine)
> Geese are ordained to bleed at Michael's shrine.

A local legend, however, would have us believe it had a different origin. According to this a Nottinghamshire farmer, who had lost his wife either by death or desertion, brought up his three sons in such complete seclusion that they grew to man's estate without once having set eyes on a woman, until the farmer at last relented and took them to Nottingham October Fair, where he asked each in turn what he would like to have bought for him. They gazed about them for some minutes, then picked out three young ladies in white dresses.

"What are those," they asked.

"Pho!" exclaimed the farmer, "those silly things are geese."

"Then," cried the three sons together: "father, buy me a goose."

When Nottingham Goose Fair was in its glory, and lasted for twenty-one days, there was no need to speculate on the origin of its name, because then upwards of 20,000 geese, each flock attended by a goose-herd with his crook, would be driven through the Goose Gate from Lincolnshire and the Fens to be sold in the market place.

Leicester had its weekly markets at the fine Elizabethan High Cross and several fairs, which are described by C. J. Billson in *Mediæval Leicester*. They are especially interesting because the most popular of them were people's fairs from the beginning. The great fifteen-day fair originally held in June, which was moved by Henry III to February—The Feast of the Purification and the fourteen days following—has a charter addressed not to the earl but to the "good men of Leicester"—*probis hominibus*. The best-known Leicester fairs, however, were those held in May and October in Humberstonegate. These were discontinued in 1902 and the owners of the old fairground compensated for their lost rents; but they are still remembered by the older inhabitants for their opening procession to which colour was added by the local waits and a contingent of old men from the Trinity Hospital, having rusty helmets on their heads, and breastplates fastened on their black taberdes.''

Processions were a feature of Midland fairs. There was Lady Godiva's, of course, at Coventry, introduced in 1678, and last held in 1870. Wolverhampton paraded the bounds on the eve of its July Fair, and in this procession there were, as at Leicester and many other places, the town's musicians attending the steward of the Deanery manor and the principal inhabitants of the town. This "walking the fair," as it was called, was discontinued at Wolverhampton about 1789. Other places in Staffordshire where the custom was observed are given by C. H. Poole in his *Customs of the County of Stafford.*

At Lichfield Whit-Monday Fair there were two special events: the procession of mechanics, each of whom carried a working model of the machine he used, and the Green Bower Feast described by Celia Fiennes, who says: "They have in this town a custome at Whitsontide the Monday and Tuesday call'd the Green Bower Feast by which they hold their Charter;. the Bailiff and Sheriff assist at the Cerimony of dressing up Baby's with garlands of flowers and greens and carry it in procession through all the streetes and then assemble themselves at the Market place and so go on in a solemn procession through the great streete to a hill beyond the town where is a large Bower made with greens in which they have their feast; many lesser Bowers they make about for the conveniency of the whole company and for selling Fruite Sweetemeetes and Gingerbread which is a chief entertainment." The Bower at Lichfield is now a pleasure fair with all the usual stalls, swings, and roundabouts; but it still has its procession with tableaux, trade exhibits and so forth, and in the late afternoon the children are given Bower cakes, which introduces the topic of special dainties prepared at fairtime to relieve the monotony of the usual diet. At Wellingborough, another Midland town with several fairs, the special dish at St. Luke's Fair was Hock and Dough Flake, which seems to

140

# Bedford

have been pork, mixed with potatoes and seasoned with herbs, encased in dough to form a kind of pudding or dumpling. On the eastern fringe of the Midlands, whirlin cakes were made for the Careing Fairs, held after Careing Sunday, or Passion Sunday, the fifth in Lent:

> Care Sunday, care away,
> Palm Sunday, and Easter day.

The great Michaelmas Fair at Bedford has always been renowned for the sale of warden pears, which have been cultivated in the county for centuries. In the old days they were baked and sold at the fair to the cry:

> Smoking hot, piping hot.
> Who knows what I've got
> In my pot?
> Hot baked wardens.
> All hot! All hot! All hot!

This Michaelmas Fair at Bedford was unquestionably the best in the south Midlands for every kind of marketable produce. "Here," says Defoe, "is the best market for all sorts of provisions that is to be seen at any country town in all these parts of England; and this occasions, that tho' it is so far from London, yet the higglers or carriers buy great quantities of provisions here for London markets. . . . Here is also a great corn market, and great quantities of corn are bought here, and carry'd down by barges and other boats to Lynn, where it is again shipp'd, and carry'd by sea to Holland: the soil hereabouts is exceeding rich and fertile, and particularly produces great quantities of the best wheat in England, which is carry'd by waggons from hence, and from the north part of the county twenty miles beyond this, and to the markets of Hitchin and Hertford, and brought again there, and ground and carry'd in the meal (still by land) to London."

The variety of fairtime customs found in the Midlands is at first surprising in view of the strength of Puritanism in these parts. Most of them, however, cannot be traced back beyond the Commonwealth, and it does seem possible that their variety is in fact due to the suppression of the more

141

regular customs and ceremonies which survive in the Catholic west and north of England, giving rise to compensating festivities, which in time themselves became established customs, just as when holy wells were discredited as such they became wishing wells. We think of such customs as that associated with Corby Pole Fair, held only once every twenty years at Corby, near Kettering. The next, incidentally, will be due in June 1962! The custom there is for a toll of not less than sixpence to be demanded of everyone entering the village under threat that defaulters will be carried shoulder high through the village in a chair set up on poles, to be put in the parish stocks.

At one time the Midsummer Fair at Boughton Green in Northamptonshire was like a county agricultural show, or rather an inter-county show, because one could find there wooden hoops from Buckinghamshire, willow bowls from Leicestershire, taps, spoons, and carved ware from King's Cliffe—once famous for its wood turners—as well as rakes and shafts from Corby and Geddington and, of course, Banbury cakes in plenty. The first day was for trading; on the second the gentry attended to raffle and see the shows, afterwards adjourning to the "Red Lion" at Northampton, four miles away, for a summer ball. The third day was reserved for wrestling and trials of skill at single stick for such prizes as a gold-laced hat worth a guinea, or a pair of buckskin gloves.

Such sports were always popular at country fairs, and were sometimes enlivened by rougher sports such as shin-kicking, for which the contestants would prepare themselves for a month before the event by rubbing their shins with blue vitriol to harden them. And, of course, mops, or hiring-fairs were always popular in the Midlands—more popular, in fact, than they were in the north and west because communications were so much better, and consequently the people were more sociable. As the inns were quite unable to cater for the sudden increase in population on these occasions, cottagers were allowed to sell beer at fairtime provided they put green boughs—usually oak boughs—over their doors, while ostlers were allowed to take in the horses of visiting farmers if they fixed a wisp of hay above the stable door.

142

## Stratford Mop

After the industrialization of so much of the area, mops provided popular excursions from towns. This was particularly so at Stratford-upon-Avon, which had the most popular of all the Midland mops. Not only was an ox roasted whole each year in front of the Garrick Inn and a number of pigs in the main street, but most of the innkeepers roasted carcases privately in their yards, or on their great kitchen spits, to supply the needs of the Birmingham pork and bacon-eaters. So popular did the Stratford mop become that the *Stratford-upon-Avon Herald* for Friday, 15th October, 1937, reported that thirteen mayors of Midland boroughs had attended the opening ceremony that year, and had afterwards visited the sideshows, patronized the roundabouts, and given their blessing to the ox-roast. Nor had they missed the opportunity to "say a few words" on so "auspicious an occasion."

The truth is that most of these Midland mops were ruined by the invasion of rowdies from Birmingham, who in their different way were no less to be feared in the twentieth century than the Welsh had been in the twelfth. As early as 1862 Lord Lyttelton presided over a county meeting held in Worcester for "the suppression of Mops," and that and similar meetings led to the establishment of "Servants' Registration Societies" in towns where mops were held. In an effort to reform the existing mops, what were called "Mop Teas" were introduced to replace the drunken orgies of the previous generation.

It was inevitable that with the general improvement in public behaviour, notwithstanding the nonsense that is talked about the unruly crowds of to-day, mops and their like should go, and the Midlands for the very reasons already given for their success—accessibility, good communications, and so forth—were obviously the first to be affected when those advantages led to the region being industrialized. Here more than in other parts, towns, with their regular markets, took the place of the old fairs, and therefore here more than in other parts, fairs, no longer serving their original useful purpose, degenerated into orgies that for the most part were better suppressed. For this reason it is all the more gratifying that the one Midland town that can contain such an annual beano, Oxford itself, should retain in full vigour its ancient fair of

St. Giles, held on the Monday and Tuesday immediately following the first Sunday after St. Giles's Day, 1st September.

Oxford has other fairs. At St. Frideswide's the custody of the city was handed over, as at York, Winchester, Hereford and other places already mentioned, to the ecclesiastical authorities for the duration, the keys of the city gates being handed by the mayor to the prior; but this had dwindled to insignificance by Stuart times, as also had May Fair, granted by Edward IV to the Austin Friars, which like St. Frideswide's had come into the possession of the city. The same fate attended a fair on Gloucester Green, which had a charter granted by Elizabeth. Only St. Giles's Fair survives and shows no signs of falling into decay, although we may be sure the older people will tell you that it is not what it was. Perhaps the most delightful description is that of Canon H. C. Beeching published in *Provincial Letters* (1906):

"The fair is held, as all the county of Oxford knows, on the first Monday after St. Giles's Day, and on the broad space in front of St. John's College, which as lord of the manor receives a moderate rent from such owners of booths as squat upon the college property, while the city takes toll of the rest. . . .

"In old days one of the most interesting features of the fair beyond question was the ghost, which as an old Doctor of Divinity used to say, was a standing witness to the supernatural. . . . It is good for us all now and then to get back to mother earth; and for no class of men is it so necessary as for those who live among ideas, like the fellows of Oxford colleges. This, with their usual wisdom, they recognize; and one of the most captivating sights of the fair in old days was the sight of the Venerable —— of —— throwing for cocoa-nuts. To anyone who was incautious enough to recognize him on such occasions he would say, 'The Romans, sir, were an imperial people: and they knew the value of the Saturnalia.' Never, too, shall I forget the spectacle of a Professor of Ancient History upon the switchback, being borne aloft and swept down again in a state of apparently frantic happiness. On that occasion our eyes met, and when he joined me subsequently he explained that, being engaged upon a description of Hannibal's passage of the Alps, he was endeavouring to

## St. Giles's Fair, Oxford

gain local colour by a substitute for the exhilaration of high mountain air." No doubt they were a couple of humbugs who thought of the reasons afterwards; but the account is none the less charming for that!

At Oxford, as the Provost of Worcester has reminded us in his recent book, *To Teach the Senators Wisdom*, you might see a luminary of the university "in the scarlet robes of a Doctor of Divinity . . . proceed through Gloucester Green to carry out his duties as Clerk of the Market. How right it was," remarks the provost, "in Oxford if nowhere else, that a Doctor of Divinity, appropriately clad, should inspect the weighing of butter and beef!" And we shall never forget that it was a Cambridge professor who gave a voice to the lads who:

> Would take the Ludlow road;
> Dressed to the nines and drinking
> And light in heart and limb,
> And each chap thinking
> The fair was held for him.

But for the best description of a Midland fair we must go, to the Poet Laureate, steeped as he is in Midland lore.

"The square," he says in *The Hawbucks*, "was crowded with the booths of merchants, most of them selling crockery, decorative china, usually pink and gold, or cakes, fruit and hard-bake, all three glistening with stickiness. Some booths sold linen shirts and cloth caps. Four shows were busy; a merry-go-round with a steam organ which played 'White Wings'; a smaller merry-go-round, with a steam organ and cymbals, which played 'Cheer, Boys, Cheer'; a smaller merry-go-round, with a trumpeter and drummer, who played what sounded like selections from 'Annie Laurie,' and a double stand of swingboats in full swing, with the swingers singing to all three. Further along were rifle saloons, with their noise of spitting, cracking, and tingling; Aunt Sally shies, with their men bawling:

> Rollo-bowlo-pitch.
> Three shies a penny at your old Aunt Sally,
> For a coconut or a good cigar,
> For a good cigar or a coconut,
> Come rollo-bowlo-pitch,

145

and the yell of a cheap-jack who stood on a wagon selling pudding-basins which he smashed to fragments from time to time when bidding was slack. "Tuppence the basin," he was shouting. "All-English pudding-basin for anybody's beef-steak and kidney pudding; come, tuppence, or I'll smash it, tuppence, or I smash it. What, you won't pay tuppence? You shan't have it cheaper. The all-English pudding-basin was used in our Royal Queen Victoria's kitchen at Windsor Palace. Windsor! Who says tuppence? Who says tuppence? Who says tuppence? Well, if you won't then ... Smash"; and smash the basin went on the cobble-stones.

"It was a holiday in Hilcote and the district near-by. The yards of all the inns were full of the traps of farmers: all the square was crowded. In the northern side of the square, close to the church, there was a hiring stand, where a few men and women hung about still, hoping to be hired; usually they were what were known as the Hilcote Hard Bargains, who had not been able to get along with those who had hired them there at Michaelmas. George had a look at them.

"Further along the same pavement there were booths (as there had been for three hundred and fifty years) for the sale of country things and country skill. A man sat there mending china, using the dancing-ball drill of Ancient Egypt, and sometimes inviting his watchers to try if they could work it. A woman, a little further along, mended rush-bottom or straw-bottom chairs while the owners waited. A turner sold the wooden cups and plates which he had made: these were still used by the very poor, though cheap tin had marred the market for them. Near him two women offered lace, once much made thereabouts, now falling out of life as fingers and eyesight failed among the makers. Another woman sold the old original Hilcote pies, being the boat of St. Nicholas in ginger-bread, stuffed with currants and spice. When George reached this part of the square the shows were lighting their flares and the women at the booths their lanterns, so that a warm light, as well as the glow of sunset, fell upon flowers and faces." [1]

[1] Quoted in Walbank, *The English Scene*, Batsford.

## Fairs in the South

While London factors and merchants must always have attended fairs in every part of the kingdom, it was only by slow degrees that provincial merchants reached London. Many, however, reached Barnet, the first stopping-place out of London on the old North Road and therefore a town full of inns, with stabling for horses and beds for the country folk, who gave colour and virility to its great September Fair, to which for more than 700 years cattle and horses—particularly colts and ponies—have been brought from as far west as Ireland and as far north as Scotland. As late as the nineteenth century Dickens could say in *Oliver Twist* that in this town every other house was a tavern.

At the time as many as 40–45,000 head of cattle came under the auctioneer's hammer each year on the great fairground that covered the hill as far as the commons to the west and north—to the site, that is to say, of the 1471 Battle of Barnet, in which the Lancastrians were totally defeated and Warwick slain. There were separate fields for cattle, horses, and sheep. And at the same time horse races were run in a field that is now the site of High Barnet station, which, incidentally was built in 1871, the year when the races were discontinued. It was Barnet Races that made the fair a favourite resort of the London costermongers and rowdies, and therefore a perfect subject for Rowlandson, who afterwards followed the crowd to Harlow Bush Common, where the unsold stock from Barnet was sold off, as the unsold stock from Brough Hill Fair was sold off at Romaldkirk.

Barnet Fair is still the most racy event of its kind near London. Even in 1952 620 horses were sold, including 74 sturdy Welsh cobs from Glamorgan, most of which changed hands within a couple of hours.

Barnet is also the site of the historic market granted by Henry II to the abbots of St. Albans described by Thomas Heywood in the *English Traveller*:

> This Barnet is a place of great resort,
> And commonly upon the market days
> Here all the country gentlemen appoint
> A friendly meeting; some about affairs

147

Of consequence and profit—bargain, sale,
And to confer with chapmen; some for pleasure,
To match their horses, wager on their dogs,
Or try their hawks; some to no other end
But only meet good company, discourse,
Dine, drink, and spend their money.

The scene at Harlow, which, like Barnet, is now turned over to builders, was much the same. Mr. Chisenhale-Marsh, writing as an elderly man in the *Essex Review* in 1896, said he could remember the fair as still a smart occasion, with all the gentlemen of the neighbourhood attending a public dinner in the afternoon. It was abolished in 1879, when the Secretary of State authorized the two most influential gentlemen in this part of the county, Mr. Arkwright of Mark Hall and Mr. Percy Watlington, to keep the common clear for the use of commoners and, if necessary, to send their men to remove any caravans or booths which the showmen might set up, with the police standing by to take action if there should be a breach of the peace. Thus Harlow Bush Fair came to an end, and the cockneys of north London had to look to Hampstead and Pinner, which as pleasure fairs still stand in the same relationship to each other as Barnet and Harlow in that from Hampstead Heath the fair folk move into Pinner High Street at Whitsuntide with their booths and roundabouts, with the result that these lively examples of ancient fairs in modern dress, adorned as they are with all the spangles and trappings of the traditional fair and with pearly kings and queens to lead the revels, preserve in the twentieth century the spirit of Dickensian Greenwich and of the immemorial Bartholomew.

West of London there were the ancient fairs of the little Berkshire towns, with Newbury boasting that its Bartholomew Fair, which like Barnet's has been held at the saint's feast Old Style since the reform of the Calendar—that is to say on the 4th September—is one of the oldest in the kingdom. It was, in fact, granted to the hospital by King John in 1215, and the profits are still divided between the seven brethren and the seven sisters living in King John's Almshouses.

At one time Newbury had eight fairs, including a July cherry fair. The busiest was the Michaelmas mop, of which a witness at the Royal Commission's inquiry in 1888 said that it used to be a great trysting-place for friends and relations in farm and domestic service all over the region, who made a point of being in Newbury on fair-day. And as it was the custom to hold back part of the wages of those in service until Michaelmas, all had money to burn holes in their pockets that day.

In this part of the country we are fortunate in having a first-hand account of old-time marketing quite uncoloured by genius or literary art in *The Reminiscences of William Clift of Bramley*, who is describing what happened about 1840:

"When I was a lad at home," he writes, "my brother Thomas had to take the corn to Reading Market on Saturdays, from Michaelmas to Christmas; the best team had to go with a 'carriage' of corn (that is, a four-horse load of ten or twelve quarters). My brother used to get his food put up on Friday, ready for Saturday; it was packed in a large basket. On Friday night the waggon was loaded, drawn out, and clothed down; care being taken to leave the waggon on a good piece of ground, so that they might have a good start. At about 12 o'clock midnight they began their journey, reaching Reading about six in the morning. I believe the carters used to take most of the harness off, on arrival, and clean their horses down, and feed them, just as they would in the morning at home. This refreshed the horses.

"A sample sack of wheat was taken out of the waggon and carried up into the Market Place, for the salesman to sell the bulk by. When sold, the carter was told to 'draw away,' that is, take it to the buyer's granary. As soon as delivery was made, the buyer was expected to pay for the corn, at the agreed price.

"This done, the carters got ready for their journey home. They generally started from Reading about 2 p.m., reaching home about 5 o'clock. As soon as they reached home, the horses were 'shot out,' and well attended to: we youngsters willingly helping, and making all sorts of enquiries as to what the carters had done and seen in Reading." [1]

West of Berkshire we run into the far-flung downland of Hampshire and Wiltshire, into the countryside of Avebury and Stonehenge, and—which is more to the point so far as

[1] Simmons, *Journeys in England*, Odhams Press, 1951.

the present subject is concerned—into shepherd's country. Here, 3 miles beyond Andover is Weyhill, a lonely village in the Downs that is the site of what was formerly the largest sheep fair ever held in England. According to Defoe—who, as his evidence is admitted to be hearsay, was probably exaggerating—as many as 500,000 sheep would be sold at a single Weyhill Fair. Others have estimated that £300,000 would change hands there at one fair. No wonder charlatans and pickpockets abounded!

Weyhill's records go back to the eleventh century; but the fair itself is much older than that. It is, in fact, the prototype of most of our ancient fairs in that, (1) it is a boundary fair, held at the meeting point of the three parishes of Amport, Monxton, and Penton-Grafton, (2) a hill fair, held near a Bronze Age barrow and at the point where ancient trackways that became trade routes intersect. Moreover, the finding of ox-teeth and other relics in the neighbourhood shows that it is a site of pagan sacrifice and festival, and the dedication of its church to St. Michael appears to be an instance of a church built on the site of an ancient fair being given the dedication of the saint whose day fell nearest to the date of the fair. And besides having a fair held at Michaelmas and a church dedicated to St. Michael, Weyhill's rector appears to have taken over the pagan priest's office of lord of the fair, because from time immemorial he has enjoyed the sole right of penning sheep on the fairground.

Further evidence for the antiquity of Weyhill Fair is found in the ceremony called "horning the colts." The colt, of course, was a person attending the fair for the first time. He was seated in a special chair at one of the village inns, wearing a cap fitted with a pair of horns. Between the horns was fixed a cup, filled for the ceremony with ale. The officiant then rose, and in mock solemnity chanted:

> So swiftly runs the hare, so cunning runs the fox,
> Why shouldn't this young calf grow up to be an ox,
> And get his own living among briars and thorns,
> And drink with his daddy with a large pair of horns?

The entire company then joined in the chorus of:

> Horns, boys, horns; horns, boys, horns,
> And drink with his daddy with a large pair of horns.

150

## Weyhill Fair

The cup was then removed and the novice forced to drink it off, after which he was expected to show his appreciation of the initiation by treating the entire company.

Cobbett, who was a great believer in fairs, uses the purchase of hunting whips at Weyhill to show how much cheaper such articles could be bought from craftsmen working at their own homes in the country and selling what they made at fairs, than from those who had expensive shops to maintain in such towns as Salisbury.

At the time of Weyhill Fair assemblies were held in the Town Hall at Andover, and the entire neighbourhood was a-flutter with excitement. For a reflection of its importance in the life of the district we need only glance at the diary of the Rev. H. White, rector of Fyfield and a brother of Gilbert White of Selborne, who tells us how he bought not only his Cheddar cheese there, but also quills for his harpsichord:

"1781. October 9th. Quills. 1500 bought from ye Sedgemoor merchant on Weyhill at 1s. per hundred, the cheapest market by far. At Andover they are full three times as dear." How Cobbett would have agreed with him! But this cheapness, as economists have proved, was dear enough in the long run, involving as it did in the majority of these undercutting cottage crafts, miserable standards of living, inefficiency, and the paralysis of enterprise.

Horses also were sold at Weyhill, and the fair produced a song which seems to have parallels in other parts of the country: [1]

> Its I hev' ben to Weyhill Fair,
> An' Oh what sights did I see there,
> To hear my tale 'ud make you stare,
> An' see the horses shewing.
> They cum from East, they cum from West,
> They bring their worst, they bring their best,
> An' some they lead, an' drive the rest,
> Unto the Fair at Weyhill. Tral-lal-lal. Unto the Fair at Weyhill.

> There were blacks an' bays, an' duns an' greys,
> An' sorrelled horses, aye an' mares,
> An' pyeballed too, I du declare,
> An' more than I du know on.

[1] *Notes and Queries*, 7th Series, v, p. 352.

There were blind an' lame, an' windgalled too,
Crib-biters there were not a few,
An' roarers more than one or two,
All at the Fair at Weyhill. Tral-lal-lal, etc.

All ages too, as I'm alive,
From one to two, to thirty-five;
An' some they scarce could lead or drive,
Or on the Down could shew 'em.
There were broken-winded too, I saw,
An' some for panting scarce could draw,
An' there were clickers too, I knaw,
All at the Fair at Weyhill. Tral-lal-lal, etc.

Now some upon the road were shewn,
An' other found upon soft ground;
An' up the hill their heads were turned,
An' that's the way to shew 'em.
They can gain or lose an inch or two,
Oh yes, they this, an' more can do,
To find the sort that will suit you,
All at the Fair at Weyhill. Tral-lal-lal, etc.

The dealers through the Fair do splash,
An' swing around a long whiplash,
An' say "My lads, come stand a-swash,
An' let's hev' room to shew 'em."
They crack their whips, an' curse and swear,
An' cry, "My lads be of good cheer,
For this, My lads is Weyhill Fair.
Howdy like the Fair at Weyhill?" Tral-lal-lal, etc.

In Weyhill and Winchester then, Hampshire had two of the great historic fairs of England. After these in importance, and not far behind them at one time, came Portsmouth's original fair, with a charter granted by Richard I, which was opened at midnight on the 9th July with the ceremony of the glove, already referred to in connection with Chester and Liverpool, and to be met with frequently in the West Country. Portsmouth's glove was stolen in 1840 and sent to America; but this removal of the symbol did not, as the purloiner believed it would, suspend the fair. Another was bought by subscription, this time one that was very definitely a hand, with the wrist in gilded mail and on the forefinger a ring bearing the device of Richard I—the crescent and seven-rayed star which are also the arms of the borough. The hand, however, was little used, for in 1846 the Portsmouth Fair was officially abolished, although the townsfolk, not to be denied their fun and games, kept a pleasure fair going. Trinity Fair at Southampton is one on which further useful research might be done by a local antiquary to follow up Mr. Crawford's article in the *Proceedings* of the Hampshire Field Club and Archæological Society. In view of its site it is probably a fair of great antiquity, and much older than the charter mentioned by Mr. Crawford as the earliest that had been discovered when he wrote. Another ancient Hampshire fair about which more information would be welcome is the one formerly held at a place called Strete—granted to a William Briwere, to be held on his manor of King's Somborne —because this was held near the much-used ford over the Test, on the Roman road running through Salisbury and Winchester to the lead mines of Somerset. Apart from these ancient fairs about which speculation would be dangerous until more data are available, all the old towns of Hampshire had their fairs, many of which survive. And as modern experiments in traditional modes of marketing, there are such delightful scenes as that in the yard behind the White Horse at Romsey, as well as others organized by the Hampshire Women's Institute.

South of London the rise and fall of fairs was similar to what it was in the north, but on a smaller scale. London was too near on the one hand, the sea too near on the other. So, with the spread of the capital, one fair after another was abolished. Croydon, for example, which at one time had several, lost its last chartered fair in 1871. Cheam, however, as a contribution to the 1951 Festival of Britain, revived its charter fair on the site on which it had formerly been held for 700 years. All these fairs near London became saturnalian events and little more in the early nineteenth century, and most of them, it must be owned, were by no means respectable earlier. Great Bookham's fair, for instance, is described by Richard Flecknoe in his *Diarium* of 1656 in the lines beginning

Through Leatherhead went to Bookham Down,
Where fair was kept of great renown,

and Flecknoe, whether priest or not, was more interested in sinners than saints.

Chertseys' two fairs, Black Cherry Fair, held on the 6th August, and the Goose and Onion Fair, held on the 25th September, were popular events in the old days. But the historic fairs in this part of the country were those along the Pilgrims' Way, in particular Shalford Fair, near Guildford, another instance of an ancient fair near a ford. Guildford's own fairs were either granted or confirmed by Richard II in the first year of his reign. Farnham also had its mediæval fairs, granted in 1247. Better known, however, was its corn market, described by Defoe as being "without exception the greatest corn-market in England, London excepted." Dorking, as we are reminded on entering the town to-day, has long been famous for its poultry—the fattest geese and largest capons, says Defoe, being reared in the neighbourhood and sold in Dorking market to the poulterers from Leadenhall. Its lamb fair, held on Holy Thursday, was also renowned.

The Surrey heathland, however, beautiful as it is, was never the countryside for such fairs as we find in the counties where agriculture flourished. Conditions were much more favourable in Sussex, where we find many small local fairs with ancient charters, like the one at Salehurst, chartered by Henry III in 1254, and such curiously named fairs as the "Jack and Joan Fair" at Canterbury, so called from its being a hiring fair, or "Sloe Fair" at Chichester, which takes its name from the tree that used to stand at the entrance to the field in which it had been held since the twelfth century. But Sussex has also its great sheep fairs, such as the one at Findon, which like Weyhill must go back well into prehistoric times.

An unusual Sussex fair was Haywards Heath Dolphin Fair —unusual because it was principally known as a pig fair. A. R. Pannett writing his memories of Haywards Heath Fair in the *Sussex County Magazine* of April, 1942, tells us that it was always attended by "a fellmonger, a trade now apparently extinct." The fellmonger tanned sheepskins brought to the fair by his customers, and made them up into leggings, hedging gloves, and bootlegs, which, says Mr. Pannett, "were long leggings reaching nearly to the top of the leg, and these, when adorned with bright brass buttons, were the pride of the maker and the glory of the owner." Mr. Pannett in this interesting account of a vanished fair also tells us about "a remarkably quaint and very dirty old couple whose line of business was singing and selling ballads" at the fair. These must have been late, if not the last, survivors of the traditional fairtime characters formerly so familiar at London fairs, and it would be interesting to know if any of their song sheets survive. Most of them would be lurid descriptions of murders, decorated by crude wood-cuts depicting the scene—"horribly gruesome details of the crime, finishing with the last speech and confession and the culprit standing under the gallows with his head in a bag, a rope round his neck, and a parson at his side." Others would be liable to seizure as pornographic.

But none of the south-eastern counties after the Dissolution —that is to say after Canterbury had lost its unique power of attraction—were of much account, and the description of Beggars Hill Fair, held at Bartholomew tide near Rye, found in the *Journeys of Celia Fiennes*, is probably not to be surprised at. It was well named, she says, because it was "the saddest faire I ever saw, ragged tatter'd booths and people." Happily, however, she is able to add that "the musick and danceing could not be omitted," even at Beggars Hill Fair.


IV EAST

To Essex and East Anglia the growth of London brought only prosperity. Not only were they rich in grain and stock themselves for its ever-increasing population, they had the north to draw on. One of the most eloquent expressions of the magnetic power of the capital is by the North Country writer De Quincey, who in his florid style says: "Often at great distances of two or three hundred miles or more from the collossal emporium of men, wealth and intellectual power have I felt the sublime expression of her enormous magnitude in one simple form of ordinary occurrence, viz. in the vast droves of cattle upon the Great North Road, all with their heads directed to London and expounding the size of the attracting body together with the force of its attracting power by the never-ending succession of these droves and the remoteness from the capital of the lines in which they were moving." [1] At the point where De Quincey saw them their heads were directed, in fact, not towards London but towards East Anglia, where a great proportion of the cattle eventually sold at Smithfield were first bought at St. Faith's Fair, Norwich. From there they were driven on to the Norfolk grazings to be fattened for six months before continuing their journey through Essex, where many were sold at the great fair held on Wanstead Flats.

Many writers have described this great October fair held about 4 miles north-west of Norwich, which at one time lasted for several weeks and was the greatest mart in England for the sale of Scots cattle, while of the benefit derived by these cattle from the vast East Anglian grazings we have accounts in Richard Pocock's *Tours in Scotland* and Defoe's *Tour through England and Wales*. More vivid, however, than either is Gilpin's. "Here," he says of the Norfolk grazings, "besides the cattle of the country, numerous herds of starved cattle from the Highlands of Scotland find their way. Here they lick up the grass by mouthfuls, the only contention is which can eat most and grow fat the quickest. When they have gotten smooth coates and swaggring sides they continue their journey to the Capital and present themselves to Smithfield where they find many admirers." [2]

The fair at St. Faith's had flourished since the twelfth century, and in the eighteenth had become a social as well as a commercial occasion. Silas Neville, the diarist,[3] after visiting it on the 17th October, 1783, tells us that "on the first day, if the weather is fine, it is usual for a great deal of good company to go for a frolic." He adds that there would be "quite a mall full of the first people in the country," and "many very pretty women." Incidentally, he also tells us that at the still vigorous fair in Tombland it was the custom for "Beaux and Belles" to attend before dinner, and "tag-rag and bobtail" after.

But here as in every other part of the kingdom the greatest

---

[1] De Quincey, *Autobiographical Sketches,* vol. xiv of *Works,* p. 179.
[2] Gilpin, *Observations on Several Parts of the Counties of Cambridgeshire and Norfolk, etc.,* 1769.
[3] *The Diary of Silas Neville,* O.U.P., 1950, p. 313.

fairs were earlier. The importance of East Anglia in the
Middle Ages is known to everyone. Ready access to the
Continent and the immense prosperity of its wool trade made
Norwich the third city in the kingdom, while navigable rivers
carried merchandise from East Anglian ports far into the
country to be sold at Sturbridge, St. Ives, and the rest of
them. And what richness there is in the mere recital of that
merchandise! What a wealth of records in connection with
the Sovereign's right of pre-emption and prisage—the right,
that is to say, of buying what was needed for the royal household before it was offered for sale in the open market, and of
taking without payment whatever was required for personal
use! For example:

The King to the Sheriff of Lincoln (1207)
"We command that you acquit in the fair of St. Botolph all
the great falcons which Henry de Hauvill and Hugh de Hauvill
bought for our use in that fair." [1]

St. Botolph's, or Boston, Fair was already an established mart
at the time of this reference, and in the third quarter of the
century became pre-eminent among eastern fairs, following
its adoption by the Hanseatic merchants, to whom Henry III
gave official recognition in 1259. Not only do we find that
great quantities of fish were bought regularly at Boston for
the king's use, which is what we should expect, but also that
many of the abbeys and priories of Yorkshire, as well as those
of Lincolnshire, bartered their wool for wine and groceries
there, while the noblemen of the northern counties attended
with their wives because the cloth they were able to buy at
St. Botolph's was so much finer than any that could be
woven on the looms of their own villages. As late as Mary's
reign Boston was still so prosperous that it was able to send
seventeen ships and 361 men to the Siege of Calais. But the
prosperity of Boston, like that of so many towns dependent
on fairs, did not long survive the Dissolution, and after having
paid more duty on staple commodities than London at the
end of the thirteenth century, and having continued to flourish
throughout much of the fourteenth and fifteenth, its trade fell
away so rapidly that by the seventeenth it had become a
decayed and ruined port.

[1] Cal. Rot. Lit. Claus. (Rec. Com.), 1, 85.

Fish was far more important as food in the Middle Ages, of course, than in times when meat was both abundant and permissible all the year round. And Boston was not the only great fishing port in the region. There was Yarmouth, whose initial rise was entirely due to the prosperity of its herring fair. Speed, in his *Historie of Great Britaine* (1611), says: "There is yearly in September the worthiest herring fishery in Europe, which draweth great concourse of people, which maketh the town much the richer all the year following, but very unsavoury for the time." In times when nostrils were not over-sensitive and stomachs not over squeamish, the profits, we may be sure, were ample compensation for the stench. Moreover, when restrictions on trade crippled all who did not enjoy the benefit of charters, patents, or monopolies of one kind or another the freedom of the herring fishery afforded unique opportunities for enterprise.

The first three weeks of the fair were filled with ceremony and feasting. The bailiffs appointed by the barons of the Cinque Ports—usually seven in the early centuries, but the number varied—entered the town on Michaelmas Eve behind four serjeants, the first two bearing white rods, the third a banner charged with the arms of the Cinque Ports, the fourth a French horn, and, accompanied by learned counsel and a jailor, proceeded to a house reserved for their use. There they were waited upon by the local authorities and invited to an eve-of-the-fair dinner. The following morning they attended divine service at the parish church to hear a blessing pronounced on the fair, and from the church went on to the toll-house, where the oath was administered to the officers of the fair.

Yarmouth Herring Fair might continue for as long as forty days. While it lasted hauls could be brought in from the cobles of the North Sea fishermen and the barks of the fishermen of Kent and Sussex, with no more restrictions than were essential for the preservation of peace and the prevention of disease, and hardly those at times. There was little restraint on either self or civic indulgence, for the fair court, called the "quest of the free fair," for which six men were summoned from Yarmouth and six from the Cinque Ports, while empowered to take tolls and impose fines, was forbidden to take anything from such people as "minstrels and women of pleasure frequenting the fair."

In return for the civilities shown them the bailiffs of the Cinque Ports kept open house, for which they had come prepared with sixteen or eighteen hogsheads of the most excellent beer, and the climax of the festivities was reached in the third week, with a magnificent banquet to which everyone of consequence in the town was invited.

But it must not be thought that this good relationship remained unclouded. When Yarmouth became prosperous this annual intervention by the Cinque Ports in the affairs of the town was resented. Even in 1297, according to Holinshed, when Edward I went to the assistance of the Earl of Flanders he had no sooner landed than the men of the Cinque Ports and the men of Yarmouth fell on each other in such fury that twenty-five ships were burnt. It is true that the Yarmouth records do not confirm the number; but they are no less sensational. According to them, 37 ships were greatly damaged, 171 persons killed, and goods to the value of more than £15,000 either spoiled or stolen.

In 1357 the *Statute of Herrings* was enacted, the preamble of which shows that there was not much freedom about the fishery at that time. However, recites the act, "Our lord the king doth will, that the barons of the Cinque Ports shall cause to be kept and governed the said fair, according to the composition late made between them and the people of the town of Yarmouth, confirmed by the king's grandfather and father, and that the said barons and the bailiffs of Great Yarmouth cause to be kept these present ordinances, in all points, and to be cried every Sunday between St. Michael and St. Martin, upon pain to lose their franchise and to be punished at the king's will. And that the people of Yarmouth suffer the said barons of the Cinque Ports to govern and rule the said fair." The original terms of the Act, which are summarized in Parkin's *History of Great Yarmouth*, remained operative until modified in Elizabeth's reign, when the number of bailiffs from the Cinque Ports was reduced to two, one from the east ports, one from the west, an arrangement sustained until payment of the composition was discontinued by Yarmouth in 1756.

## Provincial Fairs and Markets

From the trading point of view the most serious set-back came with the Dutch wars, and, although the Dutch were in favour again with the accession of William III, the former prosperity was never regained. The herring fair became little more than a pleasure fair, to which, however, the Dutch came regularly on the Sunday before the fair, a day known to the people of Yarmouth as Dutch Sunday. A fleet of herring schuyts, with their yellow sails and striped pennants flying, came up the Yarmouth Roads that morning, and for the rest of the day the Dutchmen in their baggy breeches and short jackets mingled jovially with the bluff East Anglians who had collected in Yarmouth to greet them. They did, in fact, return after the Napoleonic Wars, but not on the old footing, and the custom lapsed.

Dutch influence is widespread in the eastern counties, particularly in King's Lynn, which is often compared with a town on the Zuyder Zee. The resemblance is obvious at once. King's Lynn Fair, still opened by the mayor, is worthy to be esteemed because not only had Lynn the key to the inland fairs and markets of mediæval days, but in our own time its workshops have produced the bravest of the fiery steeds and wide-eyed cockerels that rise and fall between the fluted columns of the most up-to-date merry-go-rounds. With buildings about him that might belong to the Age of Chivalry, it was perhaps easier than we might think for their inventor, Frederick Savage, to conceive such creatures. Savage gave new life to what in his day was a dying convention. If to-day we find civic authorities not only tolerating but celebrating fairs in countless towns where eighty years ago they were doing all in their power to suppress them, it is because Frederick Savage, himself mayor of King's Lynn in 1889–90, raised the status of the fairground showmen by giving them such dazzling steam-driven roundabouts to replace the shabby old turntables, slowly revolved by a desperate-looking man or an overworked pony.

Savage had been trained first as a carpenter and later as a smith, and when the fairmen asked him to repair their gear he was able to suggest many ingenious improvements until eventually, to their delight, he hit on the idea of steam-driven roundabouts, with galloping horses, three or four abreast, to which later he added cockerels. The invention was so successful

160

that it enabled him to introduce a thriving new industry to the town. Nor was the industry confined to King's Lynn. A branch was opened at Islington, near the furniture shops of the East End of London, where parts could sometimes be made more cheaply and quickly than at King's Lynn, while for the most skilled work Italians, specially brought over for the purpose, were employed.

But these lively associations of King's Lynn with the pleasure fairs of to-day are only incidental, whereas in the Middle Ages its geographical position gave it natural advantages that were unique and essential. Through its port passed all the rich and various merchandise that carried such wealth to Sturbridge, St. Ives, and Ely. But its advantages declined. Even if other forces had not killed these fairs, the coming of ships that required waters deeper than those of the Wash and the Ouse would have done so. And apart from this, there was the increasing enmity of the sea to contend with. From Elizabethan times records are abundant all along this coast of the complications arising from inroads of the sea in one place and the silting up of harbours in another. Few towns have suffered more than King's Lynn from these adverse influences. Nevertheless it is fitting that a town so rich in the lore of fairs should come first, as it does, in the showman's calendar. Its eight-hundred-year-old fair is held on St. Valentine's Day and starts the season.

The decline of King's Lynn did not come suddenly, and in any case all kinds of shipping were not affected at once. Defoe tells us that in the eighteenth century the ships of Lynn carried more coal than those of any port between London and Newcastle, and that the town imported more wine than any other in the kingdom except Bristol and London. Evidence of this prosperity is still to be seen in the size of the great vaults along the quay. The import of timber also remained possible, and some of the fairs hereabouts—Peterborough's most notably—reflect this.

When the peculiar advantages enjoyed by the region in the Middle Ages—including, of course, the importance of its wool trade—were lost, its fairs ceased to be international marts. But East Anglia's pride and detachment from the rest of the country kept the social traditions of its fairs alive, particularly at Bury St. Edmunds, where a fair had been granted by Henry I in 1135 to assist the abbot in building the church of St. James, now the cathedral. But the choice of saint had been unfortunate. St. James's Day is in harvest time, when the people are busy in the fields. So a new charter was granted by Henry III, changing the date to the 21st September, the festival of St. Matthew. Already the fair enjoyed the king's patronage. In 1231 fur-trimmed robes of scarlet and black burnet, with tunics, over-tunics, and mantles from cloth woven on the looms of Ghent and Ypres were bought for him there by William, the royal taylor. This new mark of the sovereign's favour was to make it one of the most prosperous fairs in the eastern counties.

All the conditions for a great fair had been there from the start. The superstitious regard of the people for the martyr's relics, brought to Bury from Hoxne in 903, had given the town a constant stream of pilgrims. Its market had been established before the Conquest. And both fair and market were protected from the time of King John, who forbade the holding of any fair or market within the Liberty of St. Edmund except by the abbot's consent. So powerful was the abbey from Abbot Samson's time, and so rich its lands, that at the Dissolution its manors were among those most coveted by court favourites, who eventually encircled the town and converted it into one of the most prosperous of the provincial capitals.

It was Mary Tudor, sister of Henry VIII and grandmother of Lady Jane Grey, who gave Bury St. Edmunds its most brilliant seasons. Her first husband was Louis XII of France. After his death she married the man of her choice, Charles Brandon, Duke of Suffolk, and lived with him at Westhorpe Hall, moving into Bury for the fair, at which a splendid pavilion was built for her use. The Duke, who was one of the strongest and most dexterous men in England, provided the chief attraction. He was always ready to challenge the best who came to contests in martial exercises for the diversion of the duchess and her friends, and the pageantry and excitement attending these tournaments put St. Matthew's Fair at Bury in a class by itself in the eastern counties. At one time the festivities continued for three weeks or more, with outdoor sports in the daytime followed by social assemblies in the evening.

For a reflection of Bury Fair in the next century we turn to Shadwell, who was educated at Bury Grammar School and made it the subject of a play in 1689. And these stylish scenes must have continued for another fifty years or more, with the Duke and Duchess of Grafton, or Lord and Lady Cornwallis, attending to receive on Angel Hill the compliments of visiting nobility, and the bows and curtsies of their tenants.

There were raffling-booths, the Playhouse, the Athenæum, and the shops of the London tradesmen who came to Bury regularly for the fair. The 28th September, 1730, issue of the *Suffolk Mercury or St. Edmundsbury Post*, for example, announced that "James Hebert, Mercer and Weaver, from the Red Lion and Star in Fenchurch Street, London, is come to his shop, the corner of the Cook Row in Bury, during the time of the fair, with newest-fashioned silks, &c." In the same newspaper a Mrs. Johnson, also of London, announced that she would be at her shop in Bury Fair selling "elecampane, fenugreek, pickles, and turmeric." The *Gentleman's Magazine* has numerous references to Bury Fair.

There were, of course, ladies of more doubtful character and pedigree. Perhaps the most renowned of these in the eighteenth century was a widow named Letitia Rookes, whose two daughters were used to entice customers into her coffee-house, of which the back view is represented in Warren's 1748 map of the town. In its last years the fair was banished from the aristocratic quarter of Angel Hill and confined to St. Mary's and St. James's squares, which, of course, may have been the original site—the churchyard adjoining the building for which the first of Bury's fairs was granted. The most permanent relic of Bury Fair, the bailiff's booth, where the official party, after the proclamation had been read, fed on links, as Suffolk sausages were called, remained until the nineteenth century.

The unsavoury reputation of so many fairs in their last years, and the petitions for their suppression got up, particularly after the Fairs Act of 1871, makes the presence of gentlefolk in the nineteenth century somewhat surprising. Their attendance may certainly be taken for granted everywhere at least until the accession of Queen Victoria, and in the provinces they attended until the sixties or seventies. I am told that Nottingham Goose Fair was patronized by county families until 1882, which is exceptionally late. Tennyson, in *The Talking Oak*, writes as though the custom was still common when the poem was published in 1842:

> O yesterday, you know, the fair
> Was holden at the town;
> Her father left his good arm-chair,
> And rode his hunter down.

Olivia's brother accompanied him on horseback. Then:

> An hour had past, and sitting straight
> Within the low-wheeled chaise,
> The mother trundled to the gate
> Behind the dappled grays.

Probably we may assume that the gentry, if not the nobility, continued to patronize fairs everywhere until the coming of the railways made it possible for them to visit London more frequently. Indeed, before the time of the railways few of the squire class outside the Home Counties had ever visited London at all. Such places as Ipswich, Bury St. Edmunds, Norwich, and Lincoln would give them all the society they desired, or at least all they expected. These towns had enjoyed immense prosperity in the days of great craftsman, and were full of dignified houses in which the visiting families could entertain their friends at fairtime and enjoy for a season the amenities of town. For this purpose Bury, as we have seen, was in a class by itself in this part of the country. Of the others, Lincoln and Norwich had most in common. Both had been considerable towns at Domesday, and both had enjoyed the same kind of prosperity in the Middle Ages, when Norwich had been the collecting centre for most of East Anglia and Lincoln for a vast region extending inland through Leicestershire. From Lincoln the wool was carried down the Witham to Boston, where it was sold to merchants from Cologne, Ostend, and Ypres, as well as to the Hanseatic merchants.

Of the historic importance of sheep in the eastern counties we still have reminders in the ancient fairs at Scunthorpe

and Brigg, as well as in the less ancient but no less popular
ones at Wragby and Partney, while Norfolk has its sheep fair
at Diss, and Suffolk the Lamb Fair at Ipswich on the 22nd
August, at which as many as 200,000 head would be sold at
one time.

Of horse fairs in the region we have more than one vivid
description. The most familiar is Borrow's, who in *Lavengro*
describes Horncastle Fair, granted in 1230 to the Bishop of
Lincoln to enable his lordship to maintain a residence in the
town. "I was standing on the castle hill in the midst of a fair
of horses," he says, "I had no horses to ride, but I took
pleasure in looking at them; and I had already attended more
than one of these fairs; the present was lively enough, indeed
horse fairs are seldom dull. There was shouting and whooping,
neighing and braying; there was galloping and trotting;
fellows with highlows and white stockings, and with many
a string dangling from the knees of their tight breeches, were
running desperately, holding horses by the halter, and in some
cases dragging them along; there were long-tailed steeds, and
dock-tailed steeds of every degree and breed; there were
droves of wild ponies, and long rows of sober cart horses;
there were donkeys, and even mules; the last rare things to
be seen in damp, misty England, for the mule pines in mud
and rain, and thrives best with a hot sun above and a burning
sand below. There were—oh, the gallant creatures! I hear
their neigh upon the wind;—there were—goodliest sight of
all—certain enormous quadrupeds only seen to perfection in
our native isle, led about by dapper grooms, their manes
ribanded and their tails curiously clubbed and balled. Ha!
ha!—how distinctly do they say, ha! ha!'"

It is characteristic of the East Anglian that his visual sense
is strong. And who can wonder with the matchless light he
enjoys! Beside Borrow's description of Horncastle Fair I
would set Sir Alfred Munnings's description of Lavenham
Horse Fair in *An Artist's Life*, where he recalls the thrill he
had in visiting this famous fair for heavy draught horses,
which he made the subject of one of his paintings. He describes in his racy style the prosperous confident men with fat
jowls and "John Bull" hats who came into Suffolk to buy
horses for brewers' drays and railway lorries. "I see," he says,

"the powerful quarters of those great cart-horses standing in rows in market place and yard, their manes and tails plaited with straw and braided with blue, yellow and scarlet ribbons. Their action when trotted out was as vigorous as that of the hackney. Their necks were 'clothed in thunder,' their hooves sounded in the street while a man running behind bustled them with the end of a long brass-bound whip."

Although East Anglia has remained detached from the Industrial Revolution and its sombre effects, and this detachment contributes much to its charm, its towns have not stagnated. Already in Arthur Young's time corn was being carried along the Ouse and the Humber from the farms of the Lincolnshire wolds to feed the growing population of the West Riding in exchange for Yorkshire coal. Lincolnshire was also beef-rearing country, with cattle wintered on turnips and mangolds in the great stockyards we find there, to be turned out on the marshes in spring. The Lincolnshire short-horns were well known in the eighteenth century as hardy beasts that fattened quickly. As the extensive marches along the coasts of both Lincolnshire and Norfolk have remained unsuitable for raising crops, great herds of bullocks are still fattened on them ever year, although the ground on which St. Faith's was held is now the site of an aerodrome and the fair is almost forgotten. Incidentally, another Norwich fair that was formerly of more than local importance was the Rush Fair held on the first Monday in August for the sale of candle rushes, which were cut in the Broads and peeled, dried, and bundled nearby before being sent into Norwich for sale.

Of the typical East Anglian country fair, perhaps the best surviving example is Long Melford's, at one time renowned for the fights that always broke out there sooner or later. In *Lavengro*, we remember, Borrow refers to a particular kind of blow in the fight with the Flaming Tinman as a Long Melford. No fair could have a more perfect setting, but like so many others it is not what it was. It lives, however, in a description that is never likely to be surpassed: that in Julian Tennyson's *Suffolk Scene*, where in a most thrilling passage the author tells us how he was drawn into judging between two gipsy dancers, Little Lodie, "light as a leaf and with eyes as sharp

166

and steady as a bird's," the wife of a horse-coper named Remm, a man with "a smirk on his thin, contemptuous lips," and Mary Lal, "a large woman, with a firm, swaggering figure, her black hair tangled and untidy, her handsome brown face flushed with a day of heavy drinking," the wife of Peter, who had "the baleful look of a tethered bull." When the verdict had been given, although with nothing more provocative than a nod in the direction of Little Lodie, the gipsies sprang at each other and the unwilling adjudicator was lucky to escape alive. Anyone who knows what Melford Fair was like in the old days will believe every word. Incredible as such an episode may seem to-day, not twenty years ago it might have occurred in any pub within 5 miles of Long Melford at fairtime—with one exception. There was one pub, I remember, kept by an elderly widow, in which the company never got out of hand, fair or no fair. So loyal were her regular customers that if any of these gipsy copers began to pick a quarrel they were instantly seized by two or three thick-set Suffolk farmers and pitched through the doorway.

There was another well-known pony fair at Sawbridgeworth, but south of the Stour fairs were not considerable. Essex had none worth describing in detail, popular as many of them were in their own locality, apart from those at Harlow Bush Common and Wanstead Flats, and the spurious Fairlop Fair. The explanation is simple. Essex had no shrine with miracle-working relics that could draw such hosts of pilgrims as were drawn regularly to Canterbury in Kent or St. Edmundsbury in Suffolk. Therefore, it had no great mediæval fair. But with markets the story is different. This great food-producing county has had several of the most prosperous in the kingdom. For all that, Essex is singularly poor in memorials of its markets. It has nothing to compare with the fine octagonal Jacobean cross at Wymondham, which encloses a much older cross, or with the cross at Swaffham, built in 1793 by the Earl of Oxford, with its lead-covered dome surmounted by a statue of Ceres. Its principal markets, those at Chelmsford and Romford, have in fact depended on London for their prosperity. Old Essex people still talk about the long processions of carts that went through Romford and Epping every morning with supplies for the London markets. But if Essex has no beautiful market crosses to rank with those just named, the size of its market squares indicates the business done in them. We think of Romford, in particular, with an area of about 9,000 square yards.

Although Romford's is in many respects the most interesting of the Essex markets, it has no charter. The reason for this is that it belonged to the Royal Liberty of Havering until sold by the Crown in 1829. Colchester's charters go back to Richard I. Chelmsford's first charter was granted by King John in 1198 to William de Sancta Maria, Bishop of London, whose successors in the see held it until 1545, when Bishop Bonner surrendered the town and manor to the king. Elizabeth I granted it to Thomas Mildmay in 1563, and it continued in his descendants until acquired by the town in 1874.

But market squares have been more than places of trade and public assembly, rich as the records of these may be. Penance was done in them, and that the shame might be the greater the court might order the exhibition to be made in the county town. Usually public penance was ordered in both church and market, emphasizing the reality of the union of soul and body, sacred and secular, maintained throughout the country until misguided reformers had the insolence to separate what the Creator Himself had joined. As one of the inumerable illustrations, I find here the record of an Ongar woman being sentenced by the archdeacon of Essex, on the 15th December, 1569, to do open penance in the market at Chelmsford, draped in a sheet, and there to confess her offence penitently. And the following Sunday to do the like in Ongar church.

As there is little of general interest to say about Essex fairs and markets in comparison with those of other parts, space may be allowed for mentioning a curious custom in connection with the ancient market at Writtle. "Within this maner," says Morant, "there is a remarkable custom called Leppe and Lasse; viz. That every cart which comes over a part thereof called Greenbury, except it be the cart of a Nobleman, is to pay fourpence to the Lord of the maner. It is supposed to have anciently been a market place." This fourpence, which is sometimes referred to as green-silver, would almost certainly be a market toll.

## V   WEST

Novelists have worked on the smuggling lore of the Devonshire coast, and have conjured up trains of packhorses moving
along the narrow lanes, in the cover of the high banks that
shut out the kindly Devon scene from the traveller of to-day.
But we do not forget that these same high banks gave protection to other trains of packhorses. Along these bowery
Devonshire lanes passed less romantic but no less vital merchandise: rolls of cloth woven on cottage looms, that were
sent from scores of villages and small towns to be sold in the
serge market at Exeter to travelling merchants, who sold
them again at small-town fairs in every part of the southern
counties.

The homely and picturesque character of West Country
fairs, their simple friendliness and the folk spirit that has
been preserved in them through so many centuries—the customs, songs, and beliefs of the bygone age that we call Merrie
England—have a perfectly simple explanation. The personali-
ties at these fairs were neither haughty clerics nor the
stewards of proud nobleman, but genial, stout-hearted
yeomen—Uncle Tom Cobleys—who foregathered here with
foxhunting parsons and country squires not above driving
their flocks to fair or market, and sitting down with their
neighbours afterwards to roast goose or lamb-pie washed
down with Devonshire cider. Unlike the north and east, this
was never a county of great landed families who ruled like
Norman barons, but rather, as Mr. W. G. Hoskins shows in
his *Industry, Trade, and People in Exeter*, 1688–1800, of small
esquires and gentry.

The effect of this middling society is seen again in the
history of the towns. As the incomes of the Devonshire land-
owning class were relatively small and their estates far from
London, Exeter came to be even more exclusively a provincial
capital than either Bury St. Edmunds or Norwich, from either
of which London could be reached within two or three days. In
remoteness it was comparable, perhaps, with the North Country
capitals, although even York was probably less isolated than
Exeter, because the great landowners of Yorkshire were of
higher rank and greater wealth than those of Devonshire.

Indeed if the provincial capitals were carefully studied in relation to each other it might well be found that, so far as connection with London went, Exeter was the most isolated and self-contained of them all, yet at the same time readily accessible to its satellites, as a glance at the map will show.

One of the reasons for the west being held by men of moderate means was that in the Middle Ages invaders were less to be feared here than in the north and east. Consequently, few castles were built, and few fairs were granted to powerful nobles to assist them in the defence and administration of the region. Exeter's Lammas Fair was held at one time jointly by the Earl of Devon and the Priory of St. Nicholas, but even that passed to the city some time in the sixteenth century, after the earl's moiety had reverted to the Crown in 1537 on the attainder of Henry Courtenay, Marquess of Exeter. As for the Church, there was little wealth in it beyond Somerset, and much of Somerset was either in the hands of the bishop of Winchester or subject to his control. Taunton, the county town, was his. It was to the bishop of Winchester that its fair was granted in 1256. The fairs at Bridgwater, Frome, Wells and Glastonbury, which, of course, had an abbey of immense wealth and power, were important in the county itself, but not beyond it. And as the Church retained its hold longer in the west than in the Midlands and East Anglia, the immemorial habits of the people—the folk life of the region—continued relatively untroubled by the disruption of the Dissolution in the sixteenth century and by Puritan fanaticism in the seventeenth. So we find Christian and pagan elements in fairs surviving together, and no one condemning their unholy union. Maypoles, such ungodly creatures as the Padstow Hobby Horse, and May Day ceremonies that were survivals of pagan fertility rites, remained uncensored by the majority of parsons, who were neither learned nor godly themselves.

The most notable feature of West Country fairs is the exhibition at many—perhaps most—of the hand or glove, already met with at Chester, Liverpool, Portsmouth and other places. The explanation of this curious survival, as R. Stewart-Brown points out in his authoritative article on the Chester

170

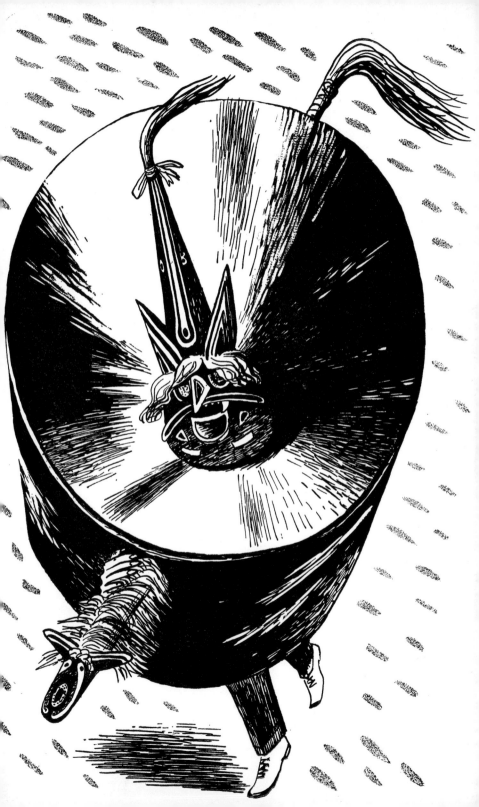

hand,[1] is found in the *Speculum Saxonicum,* a collection of German native customs, which shows that whether hand or glove it was undoubtedly used to symbolize the sign manual. Its display, therefore, was emblematic of the king's pledge to protect all who used the fair honestly and conformed with the terms of its charter. This would be understood well enough in the Middle Ages. In *Timon of Athens* the senators, before offering their submission, ask Alcibiades to send them a glove, "or any token of thine honour else."

Although Exeter's Lammas Fair, which, incidentally, takes its name from the Loaf-mass of the Anglo-Saxons—the feast of the first fruits—lapsed in the nineteenth century, the ceremony of proclaiming the fair and displaying the glove was maintained without break until the fair was revived by the Exeter Chamber of Trade in 1939 for its local shopping week. According to local tradition, the proclamation procession should start from Exe Island, where the glove was at one time kept, and proceed through the city to Southernhay, pausing at the Cattle Market, Fore Street, and the site of the old East Gate for the proclamation to be read, before entering the Guildhall, from which the glove, garlanded with flowers and ribbons, remains on show throughout the fair. But in spite of this local tradition we may be sure that the proper place for the glove to be kept is, and always was, the Guildhall. Certainly while the fair was in abeyance it was from the Guildhall that two Sergeants at Mace, accompanied by a drummer, a fife player, and the pole-bearer who carried the pole to which the glove was fixed, set out to proclaim the fair that for the time being failed to materialize. Just why it should have fallen into disuse is not clear. The local story is that it was abandoned after a farmer from the Crediton district had been robbed and murdered in Exwick Fields on his way home. But then Crediton always did tell tales to the discredit of Exeter—inspired, no doubt, by jealousy. Is it not claimed that

> Kyrton was a market town
> When Exeter was a fuzzy down?

Whatever in the past may have been the local interest in this ceremony of the glove, we may be sure that to-day it is

[1] *Chester Arch. Soc. Journal,* vol. xx (1912).

maintained, and quite properly, as an attraction to visitors, which means that to be effective it must occur in the holiday season. So Exeter Lammas Fair is no longer held at the appropriate time, but on the Tuesday before the third Wednesday in July.

One town, Honiton, maintains this picturesque custom even more vigorously than Exeter. This pleasant old town, known for its delicate lace, has a fair granted to Isabella, lady of the manor, in the twelfth century. Whether as at Ely the lace and the fair are connected or not I do not know, but its saint is St. Margaret, whose day—conveniently—falls in the holiday season. So on the first Tuesday after the 19th July the town crier in his cocked hat, wearing a blue and scarlet cloak trimmed with gold lace, proceeds along the broad main street of Honiton, proudly bearing before him a garlanded pole with a gilded glove at the head, crying:

> Oyez! Oyez! Oyez! The glove is up! the glove is up!
> The Fair is Open! God Save the Queen!

The ceremony thus completed, the hand or glove—whichever you prefer to call it—is set up over the porch of one of the principal inns, and hot pennies are thrown from the windows. On the second day it is moved to another inn, and again hot pennies are thrown. These pennies, once so precious, are heated on a shovel, and if the children are wise they take the precaution of splashing them with water before picking them up. But this takes time, and the artful may grab the pennies that others cool, or the water may be wasted. The fun, therefore, is in watching the greedier children dancing about with burnt fingers, and is yet another example of the cruelty, however mild in this instance, that has always tended to be present in mass celebrations.

Although Honiton Fair is largely a pleasure fair now, store cattle and ponies—perhaps equally to the entertainment of visitors—are still sold there.

Other West Country towns have their own ways of welcoming and entertaining the visitors from whom the people of Devon especially derive so much of their income. At Torrington May Fair, for example, which was attended recently, I noticed, by the Lord Mayor of Plymouth and the mayors of

## Widecombe Fair

Exeter, Torquay, Barnstaple, Bideford, South Molton and Okehampton, as well as the heads of other local authorities and public bodies, visitors are greeted with a large banner across the square, bearing the greeting:

Us Hopes You'll Enjoy Yersell an' Us be Plaised to Zee 'ee

Of all these popular West Country fairs it is Widecombe's that draws the biggest crowds, although—be it whispered—Widecombe Fair has been stated on what is apparently good authority to be only a hundred years old—to have been founded, to be exact, on the 25th October, 1850. Although enough ponies and sheep from the moors are sold here to give visitors their money's worth, it is the song that makes Widecombe famous, and its principal exhibit is neither a charter nor a glove but an entry in the Parish Register of Spreyton Church: "Thomas Cobley, aged 96, was buried March 6th, 1794." But what this Thomas Cobley of the eighteenth century had to do with a fair founded, apparently, fifty-six years after his death must be left for West Country historians or antiquaries to explain!

But modern or not, Widecombe Fair does meet a need by its sales of Dartmoor ponies, and has more of the character of a traditional country fair than many with longer pedigrees. Dartmoor ponies are also sold at Okehampton, Princetown, and South Brent, all of which have increased in importance with the growing popularity of pony clubs, and may be compared with the sales of New Forest ponies at Lyndhurst and Ringwood, and of Exmoor ponies at Bampton, one of the real, honest-to-goodness fairs of the west, as well as at several other places.

Folk songs connected with fairs are to be found everywhere in the West Country. One of the best, surely, is Bridgwater's, which goes:

> The lads and lasses they come through
> From Stowey, Stogursey, Cannington too.
> The farmer from Fidlington, true as my life,
> He's come to the fair to look for a wife.
> O Master John, do you beware,
> Don't go kissing the girls at Bridgwater Fair!

## Provincial Fairs and Markets

There's Tom and Jack, they look so gay,
With Sal and Kit they haste away
To shout and laugh and have a spree,
And dance and sing right merrily.
　O Master John, do you beware,
　Don't go kissing the girls at Bridgwater Fair!

Song and dance have always been typical of West Country
fairs, along with what in later times has seemed like noise for
the sake of noise. But was it always so meaningless? One of
the rowdiest fairs in the west is Pack Monday Fair at Sherborne, which according to tradition was started to celebrate
the completion of the abbey church of St. Mary on that day
in 1490 by Abbot Peter Ramsam and his workmen. It was
the day, therefore, on which the workmen packed their tools.
But this romantic origin is more than doubtful. Pack Monday
Fair is held on Old Michaelmas Day and appears to date back
to the reign of Edward I. We could hardly imagine Sherborne
having to wait until 1490 for a fair. It had, in fact, three in
the Middle Ages: a July fair which came to be called Castle-
town Fair, one at the end of December called the "Fair on the
Green," as well as this fair at Michaelmas. This is not to say,
of course, that the nave was not completed on that day.
What more likely than that the abbot should have aimed at
completion by fair day, from which every event in the year
was dated in those days? And if the work was done to time,
what more likely than that the workmen should celebrate
their achievement so merrily that Michaelmas Fair at Sherborne should afterwards be known as Pack Monday Fair?
But what of the noise? It is provided by "musicians" called
Teddy Roe's Band, which to-day are a company of boys and
girls who on the eve of the fair link arms and rush madly
through the streets, blowing horns or tin trumpets, and
rattling tin kettles, or anything else that will make a noise
strident enough to scare the devil himself—which, may, in
fact, be the original purpose of it.

One theory of the origin of Teddy Roe's band is that it
was started by the procession of workmen, led by their fore-
man, whose name is surmised to have been Teddy Roe,
rattling their tools as they marched through the town to
proclaim the completion of their work. But would this be

176

done on the eve of the fair? And in any case, it is surely highly probable that the band goes back earlier than 1490. If so, two explanations become probable, with preference to either the one or the other according to the antiquity of the band, which it is no longer possible to determine with anything approaching accuracy. The one explanation of its rowdiness is that it was started to guide travellers across the moors, a purpose it would undoubtedly serve; the other is that it had its origin in the frightful noises made in early times to banish evil spirits on the eve of a pagan festival. Bonfires were used for the same purpose in both the west and north. And bonfires were originally bone-fires, which again may have had one of two origins, according to their antiquity. Either they were started as signals, or they were originally funeral pyres on the sites of our oldest fairs, kept up in early times to celebrate the battle in which the hero was slain, and in later times to serve a more utilitarian purpose.

In these speculations we come perilously near to opening up the folklore of fairs, a fascinating subject that would lead us into a labyrinth from which it might be difficult to escape. Yet we cannot by-pass the subject entirely because Teddy Roe's band and similar hullabaloos elsewhere may well have been related to what in the north is called "riding the stang," in Devon "skiverton riding," which was an accepted method of establishing fairs. According to correspondence in *Notes and Queries*, 26th August, 1854,[1] at least four Devonshire fairs were founded in this way. They were those at Bratton, Fleming, Chittlehampton, and Lynton. For this to be done required a jealous husband who had beaten his wife unjustly, was henpecked, unfaithful, or otherwise showed himself a weakling or a fool, to be exposed to public ridicule. This was achieved by assembling a procession like Teddy Roe's, carrying cow's horns, frying-pans, warming-pans, shovels, fire-tongs, or any of the instruments named a moment ago as likely to produce a frightening noise, which attended through the town a man dressed in women's clothes, who might be borne through the streets either on a chair fixed to poles or seated on a donkey, escorted by a man wearing a pair of ram's horns. This ribald procession perambulated the town

[1] *Notes and Queries*, 1st Series, x, p. 165.

on three successive days, and on the same days ram's horns were fixed for one hour in three adjoining parishes after due notice of the intention to fix them had been served—presumably so that objection could be made. When this had been done, the parish riding "skiverton" established, at least according to popular belief, the right to hold an annual fair. At the first of these, the tolls were offered to the delinquent husband, who was expected to refuse them. They were then offered to the lord of the manor, who thereupon became lord of the fair. It is asserted in the correspondence in *Notes and Queries* just mentioned that "skiverton riding" had actually taken place at Lynton in accordance with these rules only two months before the date of the letter, that the husband had refused the tolls and that the lord of the manor had accepted them.

This is only one of many customs linking the north with the west. In Cornwall—particularly at Falmouth and Bodmin—the most popular sport at fairs is wrestling, which is also the great sport at North Country fairs and wakes. The rules, however, differ. The hold is much less formal in Cornwall than in Cumberland.

Apparently the story of the Phœnicians coming into Cornwall to buy tin is now descredited. It appears to have been invented by William Camden. On the whole, the trading history of the Cornish fairs may be thought less picturesque than that of fairs in wealthier countries. It is certainly less important economically. The Cornish fair that does arouse more than common interest from a cursory survey—and I do not pretend to have examined Cornish fairs in detail—is that at Summercourt, which is situated at the centre of the county and at the crossing of two main roads. According to local tradition this fair was originally held at Penhale, where the glove ceremony was performed in the usual way, and its removal to Summercourt followed the theft by the people of Summercourt of the Penhale glove, which according to popular belief carried with it the fair. Whatever the truth of this may be, Penhale is itself near enough the cross-roads to leave the significance of the site undisturbed. Incidentally this is yet another Cornish fair renowned for its wrestling matches.

But we must not give the impression that the farther west we go, the rougher the people. According to that doughty old showman, "Lord" George Sanger, one of the roughest fairs in England a hundred years ago was Lansdown Fair near Bath. Bath itself had four fairs at one time. The Bishop's Fair, known later as the Cherry Fair, survived until 1851. The Prior's Fair died out during the eighteenth century, though precisely when is not known. Of the King's Fair still less is known. The Citizen's Fair, later known as the Orange Fair, continued until 1854. Sanger's vivid description of Lansdown Fair is worth quoting:[1]

"From place to place we went with our little show," he says, "and at length found ourselves at Lansdown, near Bath, for the big cattle, sheep and pleasure fair that then used to be held annually on August 10th at the hill village which is some two miles from the old city. . . . Bath at this period had in its slums what was considered to be the most brutish and criminal mob in England, and for these people Lansdown fair was, as they put it, 'their night out.'

"Though it lasted but one day, the fair was always a big one, occupying a great space on a broad hill-side. On this booths, shows, and refreshment tents of all descriptions were erected to form an enormous ring, in the centre of which were the droves of sheep, cattle, and horses that formed the staple of the fair to which the country folk flocked from all the district round. . . . As dusk came on the regular business people—the farmers, graziers, and others who had been dealing in the horses, cattle, farm produce, and such-like—left the fair to the pleasure-seekers. The drinking booths, ginger-bread stalls, and shows began to twinkle with lights. . . . As night advanced the character of the fair crowd gradually changed. It grew rougher and rougher. Fights were frequent. Oaths and screams were mingled with coarse songs from the drinking and dancing booths, which were filled with a motley throng." Then came the mob from the city. "The scenes that followed are almost indescribable. Not content with drinking all they could, the ruffians turned on the taps, staved in barrels, smashed up bottles, and let the liquor run to waste. Then they started to wreck the booths. Canvas was torn to

---

[1] "Lord" George Sanger, *Seventy Years a Showman*, p. 83.

shreds, platforms were smashed up and made bonfires of, wagons were battered and overturned, show-fronts that had cost some of their poor owners small fortunes were battered to fragments. Everywhere was riot, ruin, and destruction."

No doubt it was such scenes as Sanger describes that led to the closing of fairs in every part of the country in the eighteen-seventies, and if there were many families like the Sangers on tour it can hardly have been the fault of the show-men that they became so disreputable.

There was thus all the colour and excitement that one could desire in these West Country fairs, although it may be con-ceded that it has been for their social rather than their trade value that they have retained such a hold on the people during the last two or three generations. One, however, St. Giles's Fair at Barnstaple, which opens on the Wednesday before the 20th September and has been held continuously for 700 years, surpasses the others in most respects, and may be regarded as the most typical of the West Country fairs. Not only is it an all-round country-town fair, but it has the reputation of being merrier than most—as a reaction, it is said, against the rule of the straight-laced Plymouth Brethren, with whom the town was formerly a stronghold. At Barnstaple the glove, adorned with dahlias, is displayed in front of the Guildhall, and the proclamation of the fair is followed by a civic lun-cheon, at which spiced ale, mixed by the senior beadle from a secret recipe, is the drink, served with toast and cheese.

When we turn to the markets of the region we again find Barnstaple pre-eminent. Held every Friday, it is the largest of the pannier markets of the West Country and a sight to gladden the heart. Happily it is not the last. There are still pannier markets at Tavistock and Tiverton, and probably at other places, with the buxom farm-wives of Devon and their bonny daughters seated along rows of benches behind the trestles on which their great panniers are set—brimful of all the luscious and fragrant produce of the west: chickens, clotted cream, and all the season's yield of garden, farmyard and orchard. At Barnstaple, also, may be seen the Tome Stone, on which debts were paid in the old days, and the covered way, dating from the second half of the seventeenth century, where the market was held before the present market house was built.

Nor do we forget that this is the country of the beautiful market crosses, of which the one at Malmesbury in Wiltshire is the outstanding example in the stone region. Not all of them were for the sale of farm produce only. Perhaps the most picturesque and familiar in the west is the seventeenth-century Yarn Market at Dunster, an octagonal structure with wide, overhanging eaves, dormer windows and a lantern at the top. But most of them were for the sale of agricultural produce. In the fine old market house at Chippenham, for example, were sold cheeses produced in the rich pasture land surrounding the town. Outside Chippenham, linking the town with Kellaways, is another market memorial in Maud Heath's Causeway. Maud Heath was not the wife of a wealthy wool merchant who wished to perpetuate either her own or her husband's memory, but a poor market women who had suffered all her life from the frequent flooding of this length of road, which may often have prevented her getting to market with her produce, so in 1474 she gave her small savings for an arched causeway to be built. After her death grateful friends set up a monument to her memory on Wick Hill.

Cornwall has two surprisingly imposing market houses. One is at Penzance, and was built in 1836 of Cornish granite. It has an Ionic portico to the first and second storeys and is surmounted by a dome with Tuscan columns. The second was built three years later at Helston. It is similar to the one at Penzance, but with Doric columns on the upper floor.

So here in the west, where so much is left to remind us of the carefree customs of old England, we end our survey. Whatever our personal predilections may be, we can hardly fail to find something to quicken the imagination and bring back memories. In the great sheep fairs of Dorset, such as the one held near an earthwork at Poundsbury, as well as at others already mentioned, we sense that strange—almost eerie—survival of the immemorial past in the most prosaic incidents of the present that is so strong in the novels and poems of Hardy. Indeed Hardy wrote specifically of this mood in the poem "A Sheep Fair," in *Human Shows, Far Phantasies, Songs, and Trifles*:

> Time has trailed lengthily since met
>     At Pummery Fair
> Those panting thousands in their wet
>     and woolly wear:
> And every flock long since has bled,
> And all the dripping buyers have sped,
> And the hoarse auctioneer is dead.
> Who "Going—going!" so often said,
> As he consigned to doom each meek, mewed band
>     At Pummery Fair.

But the minor key is not for everyone's memories of these West Country fairs. For some they were scenes of rousing merriment; for most, perhaps, there was less than we suppose to distinguish them in essentials from the fairs of other regions. North, south, east, and west there was the same stir when the nobility or gentry arrived in their smart turn-outs, with harness and fittings polished as for an army parade, the family arms on the cracked but gleaming varnish of the carriage doors; then the bobs and curtsies as his lordship or Sir John stepped out to acknowledge the respects of his tenants. Booths had been set up in every available space in the village, with a large tent flying the Union Jack in the middle of the green. Every farmhouse for 2 miles or so around had been filled with visiting kinsfolk, whose gigs could be seen in the yards. In every cottage the largest ham was taken down and cooked on fair day. And last came the music and dancing that went on till cock-crow or even milking-time in the great kitchens and barns. They are heart-warming scenes to remember.

# CHAPTER VIII

# Fairs—New and Old

SUCH through the centuries were our English fairs and markets in relation to the life and character of the people who made them and were made by them. The earthworks, burial mounds, pillar stones, and curious crosses that mark their sites are more than casual reminders of their antiquity and the wealth they produced. They are the milestones of our progress before records were kept. And when records were started these showed that fairs were our first—our fundamental—school of economics, in which enterprise was put to the test and developed by experience, to the enrichment of the community until the cunning and powerful learnt the art of cornering, and by their greed destroyed their own as well as their neighbour's weal. Most of them, as we have seen, came into the hands of the mediæval Church and waxed and waned with it. But fairs in the mediæval sense remained useful long after the Dissolution, and we find Braithwaite, in setting out the qualities required in the chief officers of an earl's household about the middle of that century, saying: [1]

[1] *Some Rules and Orders for the Government of the House of an Earle,* c. 1640.

"They must be able to judge, not only of the prices, but of the goodness of all kindes of corne, Cattell, and other household provisions; and the better to enable themselves thereto, are oftentimes to ride to Fayres and great markets, and there to have conference with Graziers and purveiors, being men of witt and expereince." For all that, apart from a few exceptions, fairs on the grand scale had been in decline for a century or more, and their decay was to continue until, by the nineteenth century, most of them had become shadows —counterfeits of what they had been—notwithstanding the pleasures that country folk still found in them and the reluctance of townsfolk to let them die.

The survival of fairs, both rural and urban, is as curious and interesting as their rise and fall, and cannot be explained simply by observing that man does not quickly discard the habits and customs of centuries. There is something, it seems, in the very principle of the fair that society, for profit as well as pleasure, finds indispensable. It may be true that in the nineteenth century fairs were kept alive for the sale of livestock, and for no other purpose except pleasure: that sooner or later the traditions of craftsmanship, which apparently kept smaller fairs going in rural areas, were bound to be killed by mass-production and easier transport to towns with market halls, shops, and warehouses. In short, that the trend of social development was against them, except for the sale of livestock. And there was a very good reason for livestock having remained in a class apart. Sale by auction seemed then, as still, the best means of disposing of animals publicly, and it was already seen that these auctions should be frequent and regular. In a word, that weekly or fortnightly auction marts could do for livestock what warehouses and shops were doing for produce and commodities. But at first there was an an insuperable obstacle. Auction marts were introduced about 1836; but it was not until the repeal in 1845 of the tax on moveables and heritable property sold by auction, except when the sale took place on a farm, that it was possible for auction marts to flourish. Before then, the sale of cattle in towns was so complicated a business that there was little that the farmer could do to by-pass fairs, although by the nineteenth century the limitations imposed on him by this dependence on an annual or bi-annual fair had become almost intolerable. The farms of his ancestors had been largely self-supporting. Money had counted for little in their day. Now it had become master, and if a bad harvest, domestic trouble, or any other adversity left the farmer with insufficient capital for current needs he was obliged to sell to a visiting dealer for whatever was offered, knowing full well that if a quick survey of the farm made it plain to the dealer that the need of money was urgent the price would be dropped accordingly.

Yet just when it appeared that fairs as an institution had received their death warrant, they were suddenly revived in a new and vigorous form—indeed in several forms, which while hardly fairs in the letter were undoubtedly fairs in spirit and purpose. Most notable among these were the great agricultural shows, both national and county, of which the first was the Bath and West of England. This revival in agricultural showmanship found its strongest incentive in the benefits derived from the co-ordinating of work of the Board of Agriculture, formed in 1793. Encouraged by this revival, the Smithfield Club was founded in 1798, with the Duke of Bedford as president, specifically to encourage stock breeding and hold shows. Unfortunately the Board of Agriculture did not survive the economic depression that followed the Napoleonic Wars; but its last big effort was the holding in 1821, at Aldridge's Repository, of the first National Agricultural Show in London, and the show spirit, which was undoubtedly a manifestation of the fair spirit, took immediate hold on the people.

So much for the rural areas, where the fair had its strongest hold, but to which it was by no means confined. In urban life there was a corresponding revival in the development of trade exhibitions, for which the name "fair" is now, in fact, used. The first of these was held in 1756 by the Society for the Encouragement of Arts, Manufactures, and Commerce, and was followed by a series which culminated in the Great Exhibition of 1851, the first international fair of modern times. By the end of the century, however, it again seemed that fairs, whether in ancient or modern guise, had served their purpose. But once more the impression proved false.

When commerce had to be restored after the First World War the method of holding fairs was again and most successfully adopted, particularly in the Wembley Exhibition of 1924–5.

Thus fairs or their equivalents seem destined to continue. The British Industries Fair of to-day is neither more nor less than the modern equivalent of Sturbridge, and the wealthy industrial magnates who attend it are the prosperous descendants of Ben Jonson's "sodden North Countryman, who doth change cloth for all at the fair here." Rahere, the king's jester, who inspired the revels of "Old Bartlemy," might have been puzzled by the South Bank Exhibition of 1952, but he would soon have got the hang of things in the Festival Gardens.

The social necessity of fairs, as distinct from their commercial necessity, is obvious at once. In hundreds of places the pleasure fair has outlived the trade fair. We have lost, or are losing, delight in exhibitions of deformity; but the wild beast shows, first introduced to make real to simple peasants the wonders of the Creation still hold the young in heart, even though wonder no longer leads to worship in watching them, except, perhaps, in the artist. And what fairs still mean to the artist may be seen in almost every large exhibition. Sir Alfred Munnings has already been quoted. Augustus John and Dame Laura Knight are of the same gay company rejoicing in light, life, and colour. How often when we look at their canvases are we caught up by an old memory, enabling us to feel again, if only for a moment, the tingle we experienced at our first fair. In his book *Chiaroscuro*, Augustus John tells us what market day meant to him in youth, when the streets and squares of Haverfordwest "were full of life and movement. Noise, too, with the continual lowing of cattle, the screaming of pigs and the loud vociferation of the drovers." He describes his joy in the tramps, the cottage women, the gipsies, who "arrived on the scene with their horses and light carts. These people," he says, "interested me greatly. Those sardonic faces, those lustrous eyes, even then did cast their spell on me. We were taught to beware of the Gypsies; their habit of kidnapping children was notorious; yet they seemed to have plenty of their own. Aloof, arrogant, and in their ragged finery somehow superior to the common run of natives they could be recognized a mile off."

Yet exciting as fairs have been to us, the thrill of them in former times can hardly be imagined now. There was a time when they were the only week-day holidays in the year for most people—the only holidays, that is to say, apart from holy days. So gilds and fraternities of every kind made this their day of celebration, parading the streets with banners and exhibits in a procession led by the local band. Can we wonder that they were sometimes scenes of unrestricted license, and that what happened in the cherry orchards afterwards was frequently the subject of the parson's sermon on the following Sunday, although, if his name chanced to be Herrick, it might already have been the subject of a poem on the Saturday!

Even in recalling the fairs we knew as children we see that notwithstanding the timeless in them there is much that is dying as the result of our sophistication. It is, therefore, important that those who have memories should record something of the spirit of the fairs of fifty, sixty, or seventy years ago before it is too late. For this purpose intimate personal memories are better than contemporary accounts—memories of hearing across the fields, in the clear night air of spring and autumn, the clanging of hammers and the raucous voices of the mysterious strangers whose caravans had trundled through the streets earlier in the day, with their ragged children trailing behind. Dogs would be chained to the waggons; hens and pets of all kinds would be cooped up in baskets strapped to the tailboard. And always there were those enormous closed boxes that were the objects of our wonder, and from which strange sounds used to come whenever the procession stopped. We knew that on the morrow we should hear the blare of the organs and see the pall of smoke that hung so mysteriously about the fairground and subdued its brilliant light to a fiery glow. And what preparations there were in farmhouse kitchens while the girls washed and ironed their frocks, or in the stables, where the men were busy trimming with ribbons the plaited manes of horses, specially groomed for fair day.

Slight as such personal memories may seem against the pageantry of a thousand years, it is through them that those of us who still feel a wave of sensation at the sound of a roundabout organ, or respond with Munnings to the excitement of the living scene, can become part of that pageant—feeling with Hardy the pulse of a bygone age throbbing in our veins, and becoming ourselves as ageless as the thing we contemplate. There is hardly a circumstance about fairs, it seems, that cannot be traced back to the superstitious beliefs and practices of primitives peoples. What mysteries there are even in a piece of gingerbread! And the wonder increases the farther we go. If the coming of a few strangers could bring such excitement to us in our towns and villages, what must a fair have meant to those who lived on the lonely downs of the west—Tanhill, Westbury Hill, or Toller Down in Dorset, places of frightening loneliness for the rest of the year? Accustomed to see nothing but the far-flung downs, what a thrill it must have been to the few who lived there to open their doors one morning and see thousands of people, with flocks and herds, trailing along the old green tracks towards the pillar of stone that had marked the site of the fair as far back as man can measure, until as an old Dorset shepherd put it to me: "the plaäce be quoite blaäcke wi volk."

Yet as always with these customs that outlast the centuries, the root cause is simple enough. Fundamentally, it has always been their emotional rather than their commercial value that has given them such vigour. They served throughout ages of repression and frustration as a safety valve. Hardly a single emotional impulse failed to find some satisfaction at fairs. Greed, hunger, sex, fear, pride, aggressiveness and the rest of them all found expression in booths, in taverns, or on the moonlit heath, until their restless energy was either curbed by age or diverted into the creative channels of worship and the arts, the very flower of which sprang out of fairground dung.

# BIBLIOGRAPHY

*Supplementary to standard county and local histories, directories and almanacs*

Amery, Fabyan. Country Fairs, etc. *Trans. Plymouth Inst.*, vol. vii, 1878.

Andrews, William. *Famous Frosts and Frost Fairs*. London, 1887. *Bygone England*. Hutchinson, 1892.

Annual Register. Pickpockets at Country Fairs. *Chron.* 55, 1819.

Ashley, W. J. *Introduction to English Economic History*. Longmans, 1888–93.

Austin, W. Markets and Fairs of Luton, *Beds. Hist. Rec. Soc.*, vol. 2, 1914.

Bateson, Mary. *Records of the Borough of Leicester*. 1899–1905. *Borough Customs*. Selden Society, 1904–6.

Beddington, Horace. A Sussex Sheep Fair. *Sussex County Mag.*, 1935.

Benedetta, Mary. *The Street Markets of London*. Miles, 1936.

Bewes, W. A. *The Romance of the Law Merchant*. London, 1923.

*Bibliotheca Topog. Brit.*, vol. v, No. 38, History of Barnwell Abbey and Sturbridge Fair. 1900.

Bickley, F. B. *The Little Red Book of Bristol*. 1900.

Billson, C. J. *Mediæval Leicester*. 1920.

Bloom, J. Harvey. *Folklore, Old Customs, and Superstitions in Shakespeare Land*. 1929.

Borrow, George. *The Romany Rye*. 1857.

Bourguelot, F. *Étude sur les foires de Champagne*. Paris, 1865.

Bracton, Hy. de. *Treatise de legibus et consuetudinibus Angliæ*. Ed. with English translation by Sir Travers Twiss. Longmans, 1878–83.

Bradlaugh, Charles. Market Rights, etc. Speech in House of Commons, 1887.

British Museum. The Fillinham Collection of Newspaper Cuttings.

Brown, Jane. *I Had a Pitch on the Stones*. Nicholson & Watson, 1946.

Buck, C. H. *Faiths, Fairs, and Festivals of India*. Calcutta, 1917.

Bunyan, John. *Pilgrim's Progress*.

Campardon, E. *Les Spectacles de la Foire (1595–1791)*. Paris, 1877.

Campion, S. S. Corby Pole Fair. *Northants. Nat. Hist. Soc. & Field Club*, vol. xi, No. 91, Sept., 1902.

Chambers, R. *Book of Days*. 1864.

Cobbett, William. *Rural Rides*. 1830.

Cook, W. Victor. Chichester's Sloe Fair. *Sussex County Mag.*, 1935.

Cooper, C. H. *Annals of Cambridge*. Cambridge, 1842–1908.

*Country Life.*

Crawford, O. G. S. Trinity Chapel and Fair. *Proc. Hants. Field Club & Arch. Soc.*, vol. xvii, pt. 1.

# Bibliography

Cunningham, W. *The Growth of Industry and Commerce.* Cambridge, 1842–1908.

Defoe, Daniel. *A Tour through Great Britain.* 1724. *Complete English Tradesman, 1726.* 1839.

Dexter, T. F. G. *The Pagan Origin of Fairs.* Perranporth, 1930.

Dillon, R. C. *A Sermon on the Evils of Fairs.* London, 1830.

Disher, M. W. *Fairs, Circuses, and Music Halls.* Collins, 1942.

Dixon, J. H. *Ballads and Songs of the English Peasantry.* Robert Bell's edition, 1842.

Douglas-Irvine, H. *Extracts Relating to Mediæval Markets and Fairs in England.* Macdonald & Evans, 1912.

Drake-Carnell, F. J. *Old English Customs and Ceremonies.* Batsford, 1938.

Elton, C. J., and Costelloe, B. F. C. *Report of the Royal Commission on Market Rights and Tolls.* H.M. Stat. Office, 1889–91.

Ewing, Julia Horatia. *Six to Sixteen* (describes a visit to a Yorkshire Fair). Bell, 1927.

Fairfax-Blakeborough, J. *Yorkshire, East Riding.* Hale, 1951.

Famed First Friday Fairgoer, A. *Fairlop and its Founder.*

Fiennes, Celia. *Journeys,* ed. by Christopher Morris. Cresset Press, 1947.

Frost, T. *The Old Showmen, etc.* 1874.

Furley, J. S. *Winchester Records.* 1923.

Fussell and Goodman. 18th Century Traffic in Livestock. *Econ. Hist.* (Supp. to *Econ. Journal*), vol. 3, No. 11.

Gaches, L. *The Law Relating to Markets and Fairs.* 1898.

Goldsmith, Oliver. *The Vicar of Wakefield.* 1766.

Gomme, G. L. *Primitive Folk Moots.* Samson Low, 1880.

Gorham, Maurice. *Showmen and Suckers.* Percival Marshall, 1951.

Grafton, Richard. *Abridgement of the Chronicles of England.* 1571.

Gras, N. S. B. *The Evolution of the English Corn Market.* Harvard, 1915.

Green, Mrs. J. R. *Town Life in the Fifteenth Century.* Macmillan, 1894.

Gross, Charles. *Select Cases Concerning the Law Merchant.* Selden Society, 1908. *The Gild Merchant.* 2 vols. London, 1927.

Hardy, Thomas. *Far From the Madding Crowd.* Macmillan, 1874. *The Mayor of Casterbridge.* 1886. *Tess of the D'Urbervilles.* 1891.

Harrison, William. *A Description of England* (Holinshed's *Chronicles*). 1577.

Hartley, Marie, and Ingilby, Joan. Two Great Westmorland Fairs. *Country Life,* 18th August, 1950.

Hazlitt, W. C. *Popular Antiquities of Great Britain.* 1870.

Heanley, R. M. *The History of Weyhill.* 1922.

Henry, R. L. *Contracts in the Local Courts of Mediæval England.* 1926.

Hole, Christina. *English Folklore.* Batsford, 1940. *English Custom and Usage.* Batsford, 1941.

Hone, William. *Every-day Book.* 1826–7.

Howitt, William. *The Rural Life of England.* 1838.

# Bibliography

Hulbert, N. F. A Survey of Somerset Fairs. *Proc. Som. Arch. & Nat. Hist. Soc.*, vol. 82, pp. 86 ff., 1937.

Huvelin, Paul. *Essai historique sur le droit des marchés et des foires.* Paris, 1897.

*Illustrated London News*, Mops. 26th October, 1878.

Islington Public Library, Collection of Papers relating to Smithfield Market.

Jefferies, Richard. *Amaryllis at the Fair.* 1884.

Jessopp, A. A Fourteenth Century Parson. *Nineteenth Century Mag.*, June, 1892.

Johnson, R. *Customs of Hereford.* London, 1868.

Johnson, Walter. *Folk Memory.* Oxford, 1908. *Byways in British Archæology.* Cambridge, 1912.

Jonson, Ben. *Bartholomew Fayre.* 1614.

Joseph, Joe. *Guide and Souvenir Programme to Petticoat Lane.* 1949.

Keen, F. N. *Markets, Fairs and Slaughter Houses.* 1904.

Kent, William. *An Encyclopædia of London.* Dent, ed. 1951.

*Kentish Notebook, The,* Gloves at Fairs. vol. 2, pp. 138–52.

Kitchin, G. W. *A Charter of Edward III . . . for St. Giles's Fair.* Winchester Records Series, No. 2, 1886

Lipson, E. *The Economic History of England.* Black, 1915.

McCutcheon, K. L. *Yorkshire Fairs and Markets.* The Thoresby Soc., vol. xxxix, 1940.

Maine, Sir Henry. *Village Communities in the East and West.* London, 1876.

Maitland, F. W. *Select Pleas in Manorial Courts, etc.* Selden Society, 1888.

Marwick, Sir James D. On Early Fairs and Markets. *Proc. Roy. Phil. Soc. of Glasgow,* vol. xxxv, pp. 120–49. 1927.

Masefield, John. *The Hawbucks.* Heinemann, 1929.

Maugham, C. *The Markets of London.* Pitman, 1931.

Miller, D. P. *Life of a Showman.* London, 1849.

Ministry of Agriculture and Fisheries. *Markets of Eng. and Wales.* Economic Series, 1927.

Morley, Henry. *Memoirs of Bartholomew Fair, 1859,* 4th edn. Routledge, 1892.

Muncey, R. W. *Our Old English Fairs.* Sheldon Press, 1936.

Neely, Wayne Caldwell. *The Agricultural Fair.* Col. Univ. Press, 1935.

*Notes and Queries.*

Ogle, O. *Oxford Markets.* (In Fletcher and Burrows Coll. s. 2), 1890.

Owen, W. *Owen's New Book of Fairs.* 1856.

Passingham, W. J. *London's Markets.* Samson Low, 1935.

Paul, Sir James Balfour. The Incidence of Saints' Names in Relation to Scottish Fairs. *Proc. Soc. Antiq. Scot.* 5th Series, vol. iv, 1917–18.

Pease, J. G., and Chitty, H. *The Law Relating to Markets and Fairs.* London, 1899.

# Bibliography

Percival, Spencer. *Corby Pole Fair.* 1922.

Pettinghall, John. Of the Courts of Pypowder. *Archæologia*, vol. 1, pp. 190–203.

Phillpotts, Eden. *Widecombe Fair.* 1913.

Powell, E. J. *History of the Smithfield Club.* 1902.

Power, E., and Postan, M. M. *Studies in English Trade in the Fifteenth Century*, Routledge, 1933.

Quiller-Couch, Sir A. T. The Mayor of Troy. 1906.

Redstone, Lilian J. St. Ives, Hunts. *Vic. County Hist.*, vol. ii.

Rider, C. *Rider's British Merchant.* 1751–1800. *Sunday Morning in Leather Lane.* 1867.

Roger, J. Thorold. *History of Agricultural Prices in England*, vol. i, *Oxford*. 1866.

Salzman, L. F. *English Industries in the Middle Ages.* Clarendon Press, 1923. The Legal Status of Markets. *Camb. Hist. Jour.*, vol. ii, 205–12.

Sanger, "Lord George". *Seventy Years a Showman.* Dent, 1926.

Savage, Sir William. *The Making of our Towns.* Eyre and Spottiswoode, 1952.

Sharman, W. Old Fairs in Northamptonshire. Rothwell, 1903.

Smith, Dorothy Evelyn. *Huffley Fair.* Dakers, 1944.

Stewart-Brown, R. The Chester Hand and Glove. *Chester Arch. Soc. Journal*, vol. xx, 1912.

*Sussex County Magazine*, July, 1927; Sept. 1940; April, 1942.

Thompson, Pishey. *History and Antiquities of Boston and the Hundred of Skirbeck.* 1856. Boston Fair. *Associated Architectural Societies*, ii, p. 370.

Tupling, G. H. Lancashire Markets in the 16th and 17th Centuries. The Origin of Markets and Fairs in Mediæval Lancashire. *Trans. Lancs. and Cheshire Arch. Soc.*, vols. lviii, lix, 1935.

Unwin, George. *Industrial Organization in the 16th and 17th Centuries.* Oxford, 1904.

Usher, A. P. *An Introduction to the Industrial History of England.* Harrap, 1921.

Vellacott, C. H. Winchester, Hants. *Vic. County Hist.*, vol. v, pp. 36–41.

Walford, Cornelius. *Fairs, Past and Present.* London, 1883.

Waters, H. W. *History of Fairs and Expositions.* London and Canada, 1939.

Watkins, Alfred. *Old Standing Crosses of Herefordshire.* 1930.

Watkins, Mrs. O. S. The Mediæval Market and Fair in England and Wales. *Y Cymmrodor*, vol. xxv, 1915.

Williamson, George C. *Curious Survivals.* Jenkins, 1925.

Wimbolt, S. E. Findon Sheep Fair. *Sussex County Mag.*, July, 1927.

Wright, A. R., and Lones, T. E. *British Calendar Customs.* 1940.

Yarham, E. R. Fun of the Fair. *Country Life*, 30th June, 1944.

Zetter, G. *Évolution des foires et marchés à travers les siècles*, 1923.

# INDEX

# Index

# Index

196

# Index

# Index

# Index